*This is for all who held up a light
That I might see a path.*

The volume you hold in your hand is a new approach to Paganism drawing deeply on our shared history and the inheritors of the Celtic tradition. Unfortunately (or fortunately), we have precious little idea of what our Celtic ancestors did, much less how they worshipped their Gods. When our best ancient sources are accounts from their conquerors and oppressors and our modern Victorian sources are romantic at best and at worst, some sort of fantasy built around the made-up practices of peoples they were literally starving to death.

Yet, for many of us of varied backgrounds and nationalities, the Celtic worldview and its people hold an inexorable lure. Somehow, our souls know an answer to our searching is there.

So, then, how do we begin? Rev. Doyle wisely starts looking at the entirety of the Celtic past (pagan and otherwise) and teases out the thread of what would become Celtic monasticism. He then weaves that thread throughout modern paganism and modern Celtic Christianity and produces a living, breathing, 21st century way to deeply commune with our Gods.

In my 30 or so odd years in Pagan spaces I have always found something absent. We are very good at teaching and providing the basics (these days usually through a hopefully good book) and deeply lacking in finding depth and community. Again and again, we have heard from younger pagans about how they feel isolated with superficial practices that have no real connection to their Gods. When they attempt to connect to an organization (if there even is one) it is a clique at best or at worst not welcoming to them and the beautiful diversity of who they are. The founding of The Fellowship of the Nine Waves at the autumnal equinox 2017 was years of labor and this book is the first of its gifts. With it, I sincerely hope that pagans from all backgrounds find a way to commit to even the smallest daily practice of their faith and develop a sense of the deep wonder and peace that comes when we experience the divine in nature, in the Gods, and in ourselves. This conjures kindness, connection, compassion, and vulnerability that our faith desperately needs now. Hopefully, real community can come from this as well. Not just with the Gods but with one another.

To heal our broken world, we need first to heal ourselves. This book presents an eloquent path through the mists and to the deep heart of 21st century contemplative paganism.

In the peace of the grove,
A.R. Blackthorn, Rev.

I bathe my face
In the nine rays of the sun,
As the nine waves
Fall upon the shore.
Honey be in my mouth,
Affection be in my face,
As Bride so loved her son
And her heart broke at his falling.
All-seeing, all-hearing, all-inspiring
As the all-powers might be,
To satisfy and strengthen me.
The tongue of Ogma in my head,
The eloquence of Lugh in my tongue,
The strength of the Dagda in my body,
Be mine in the presence of a crowd.
(a traditional prayer, adapted)

Welcome to the Fellowship of the Nine Waves and a new practice of polytheistic Celtic monasticism!

This short book has been a labor of love to create and produce, but it has limitations built in, not merely by its short length but also by its scope. This is not a be-all end-all text of how to do polytheistic monasticism in a modern neo-pagan and polytheistic context. That text would, by necessity, need to be many thousands of pages long and encompass a huge cultural history and many cultural contexts. It would be a lovely and comprehensive text to read, but this book is not that.

This is a short glimpse into a culturally grounded daily practice, rooted heavily in Celtic, especially Irish and Scottish, monastic traditions and participating in a modern Celtic polytheistic cosmology. This can be adapted according to the personal needs of the reader, whether you choose to use any of my prayers in holiday or daily ritual practice or to take on the full office of the hours as a form of modern Celtic polytheistic monasticism.

I am a practitioner myself. This is a book of my monastic practice and my understanding of them. It is also a book of the practices of the aforementioned church, the Fellowship of the Nine Waves. While this book might be a little overwhelming, particularly to the reader who is not used to a regular practice of prayer (or associates such observations with non-pagan religious faiths), I have found it quite doable and deeply fulfilling. As I work full time and attend school, I suspect many others will be able to do the same, if they are called to do so.

I am not an academic scholar nor am I a dogmatic

theologian. This is a book produced from practical experience and an abiding need to share a new tradition with others who may feel called to a similar system or observance.

There are sections herein on history, cosmology, and spirituality. They are here because they inform the purpose and meaning of the practices described later. For those with deeper interests in the history and cosmology of the Celtic people or Celtic monasticism, I highly encourage you to seek out more academic texts, ones that cite direct sources.

This is not a reconstruction of pre-conversion monastic practice, if such a thing existed, but a modern 21st century creation. While I will go into the finer details later, I want to emphasize first here that we do not know much of the specifics of religious practices in pre-conversion Celtic lands, whether we are looking at continental Celts, who were conquered by the Romans, or the insular Celts, who converted before we find them textually in the medieval era. To the disappointment and difficulty of many modern practitioners, the Celts have not given us an accessible written record until the medieval period, by which point they had long been converted to first Celtic Christianity and then Roman Catholicism. Thus, we can observe culturally specific aspects of their later literature (and culture and folklore, at later points) that do not match with a homogenous understanding of Christianity, but that is not the same as directly reviving a pre-conversion practice.

Thus, I am in no way suggesting here that, for example, the Druids of the Classical era did (or did not) have a monastic practice. Monasticism is not the sort of religious or spiritual practice that would leave the kind of specific archeological evidence we look for in understanding the pre-conversion

Celts. Monasticism, particularly practices that do not rely on the sometimes elaborate monasteries of certain branches of Buddhism and Christianity, do not necessarily leave any specific archeological evidence at all. The mendicants of Hinduism, Buddhism, and Christianity would likely leave nothing at all behind but their own bodies.

This brings me to another important point. While this is, indeed, a book of monastic practice, this is not a book for those looking to imitate the imagined trappings of a Trappist monk or Theravada monk. I am less interested in the physical acoutrement of a modern American's idea of the physicality of monasticism: the young Buddhist, with a shaved head and saffron dyed robes, or the aging friar in his black cassock, his tonsured head sweating under the sun of the cloister garden.

While these are some of the practices of the Fellowship of the Nine Waves, an incorporated polytheistic neo-pagan monastic church, we do not have the ecclesiastical or social resources to provide for cloisters or the support of monasteries with people who have taken vows of silence and poverty. We do not engage in daily religious uniform, whether the tonsure of the Roman monks or the saffron robes by which we can socially identify some Buddhist monastic practitioners. This book is purely about practice: practice of prayer, practice of devotion, practice of rule. Please, enjoy this book, first and foremost. Read it openly and find what you need in it. It will not be and cannot be everything to everyone, but it is my dearest hope that it will offer something to many. This book is a gift and an offering. Please accept it as such!

Oisin Doyle, Fellowship of the Nine Waves

Kindle in our hearts, O Wonders and Powers,
The flame of that love
Which never ceases,
That it may burn in us,
Giving light to others.
May we shine forever
As holy temples
Set on fire with Your eternal lights,
Lights of gods and wonders and spirits
Now and forever.
(Prayer of St Columban of Iona, adapted)

OUR CELTIC
MONASTIC HISTORY

Monasticism, something not much touched upon in modern neo-paganism or Western polytheistic practice, has strong roots in Celtic culture, but especially among the Irish, Manx, Welsh, and Scottish. In Celtic and formerly Celtic lands, it is possible to come across the ruins of many a monastic dwelling, from the clochans, or famed beehives huts of Skellig Michael to the crumbling ruins of Hore Abbey in Co. Tipperary, during the course of a hike, vacation, or pilgrimage. Personally, I have fond memories of picnicking on a vacation in Ireland at beautiful roadside ruins.

For those who may feel a monastic calling, I encourage you to read the wealth of writing produced by modern Celtic Christians, many of whom lead monastic lives, in intentional communities or in their own homes in the modern world. In this short text, I will not be able to reproduce the wealth of information, spirituality, or points of view that their religious community has. I am simply here to show that we can have a polytheistic Celtic monasticism in modern practice. At the end of this book, I will include a number of influential modern Celtic Christian monastic texts that may be of interest to a neo-pagan or polytheist willing to take a little bit of effort to rework them to our cosmology.

Celtic monasticism, which has seen considerable revival in the late 20th and early 21st centuries in Europe and North America, varies considerably from their counterparts in the Latin and Northern European traditions with whom most Americans may be most familiar. As they were in contact with the Coptic monastic tradition and, very likely, the Byzantine tradition, they were deeply influenced by their coreligionists in these regions. They were also culturally bound and expressed a deeply profound Celticness both in their values and understanding of the world.

In our popular imagination, the word "monk" might invoke

the image of the cloistered man, living among other men with a bare cell and a strict life following the Benedictine Rule. We might imagine him with the Roman tonsure, in a black or brown cassock, perhaps brewing beer or attending to a medicinal herb garden. While this is not quite a fully formed idea of the Latin monastery, the Celtic monastic tradition is something entirely different.

Celtic monasticism, in distinct contrast, can be understood as an ascetic lifestyle for a fighting, warrior people. The ferocity and great will of the Celts, from insular Ireland to Celtic Iberia, has been noted by writers from Strabo to Yeats. Often building their intentional communities at the border of their own civilizations, on islands surrounded by the great desert of the sea, Celtic monks, both male and female, lived at the limits of the liminal world. Their virtues and prayers were still fiercely Celtic, influenced primarily by their coreligionists in Egypt and Byzantium and colored by their indigenous culture. At the edge of land, sea, and sky, they lived hallowed lives, focusing on the Otherworld and the peregrinatio, or pilgrimage.

Many neo-pagans and polytheists who have been working within a Celtic cosmology will be already familiar with the concept of the holy journey, or peregrinatio, potentially to the Otherworld but also within our own holy, earthly realm. In early medieval monasteries, where their saints interacted with our gods (or our gods became their saints), monks produced and copied profoundly spiritual records of holy people entering into the coracle, set upon the holy sea, and allowing the spirits and the Holy Powers to direct their voyage upon Their whims.

The history of monasticism in Christianity is important to

understand, especially as there are several lines which cross pollinate and influence one another throughout the past two thousand years. Although their differences are often forgotten or erased by the modern popular consciousness, the differences between Celtic, Coptic, Orthodox, and Latin monastic traditions is key for us to understand as we embark on a journey of polytheistic monasticism. If we are to build our own practices holistically, we must know our roots and, for many of us practicing neopaganism, our cultural heritage is Christianity and we must own that. Certainly the heritage and history of Celtic monasticism, as it currently stands, is Christian. In this manner, we can also define monasticism and asceticism for our own communities and cosmology, as they will be inherently different from our Christian forebears.

This section is a thoroughly Christian history of monasticism, as that has been the only form of Celtic monasticism that has left us written records. This does not mean it is without use to the modern neo-pagan or polytheist or that these early Christians were without the influence of their pre-conversion culture. They were, in fact, still thoroughly enmeshed in their native culture and indigenous folklore, a fact reflected in the literature they lovingly produced in the form of illuminated manuscripts. In fact, particularly for modern pagans who function within a Celtic cosmology, we rely as heavily, if not more heavily, on these distant monks as we do on modern, sometimes imperial revivalists and folklorists, such as Lady Augusta Gregory or Edward Plunkett.

For this reason, I request that you, kind reader, read this section, even if you have personal disagreements or potential trauma associated with Christianity. For when we read our own mythologies and retell our own stories, we are relying on these monks to share their folklore, their culture, and their indigenous gods with us. Although some find this heritage off putting, it is a worthwhile pursuit to understand the people who preserved the myths, gods, and spirits so that we, their cultural and spiritual great-grandchildren, can practice a new form of the old faiths. If only in gratitude to the holy dead, we can honor those who preserved our gods, spirits, and traditions in the best way they knew.

Many of the Celtic lands, in the early centuries of Common Era, remained unconquered by Rome and remained outside of that cosmopolitan, tumultuous empire. After official Roman conversion to pre-schism Christianity, conversion came in waves through the empire that eventually overwhelmed lands beyond these borders. Being, however temporarily, beyond the reach of the Rome, the conversion of the people outside of the borders of the Empire was often to a Christianity entirely their own. This was an era before easy communications across borders, before the printing press, and before some of these nations and cultures had their own written language appropriate to theological treatise. This meant that Christian conversion in this era could not be monolithic or to a uniform faith, although that would change with time.

For an understanding of the general timeline, Christianity is estimated to have arrived in Britain around the first or second century of the common era. Official Roman imperial conversion to Christianity occurred in the fourth century. Christianity had spread throughout this time through Britain, Cornwall, Wales, Scotland, and Ireland and they developed a semi-independent form of the faith. St Anthony of Egypt, who is considered the father of Christian monasticism, died 356 CE. St Columba of Iona, one of the most important of the Celtic monastics, died in 957 CE. The Celtic Church ceded to the Latin Rite between the seventh and eighth centuries, with some vestiges of the Celtic Church holding on until 1172 CE at the Synod of Cashel in Ireland.

While the cultural heresies that arose in Germanic and Celtic lands immediately after conversion and throughout the medieval period are a book unto itself, suffice it to say here that these new converts understood their new religion within the bounds of their own cultural contexts. Pelagius, who was perhaps the quintessential Celtic heretic, denied the existence of original sin and emphasized the value of free will. The Celtic men and women who created the monastic orders that defined Celtic Christianity were equally idiosyncratic and culturally bound.

As Christianity came to Celtic shores, the seeds of ascetic monastic life began to germinate in Egypt, Syria, and Bethlehem. Ascetic here means the deliberate practice of a rigorous life of contemplation and self-denial or will in order to achieve a state of higher spiritual communion. These early ascetics are often called the Desert Fathers (and Mothers) and have a powerful legacy in Celtic monasticism.

Some of these early ascetics, such as Symeon the Stylite, were hermits who practiced a fairly extreme form of ascetic life. According to his hagiography, Symeon lived on top of a column in what is now modern day Syria. Others became anchorites (or anchoresses) and lived in hermitage and solitude. However, even among those who practiced severe asceticism, there was often, if not always, a sense of community around them. They found silence in their cells and their huts, but the people who formed their larger community or clan were rarely too far away.

It is important for both historical veracity and the polytheistic interpretation of these Desert Fathers to note that women did actively participate in the early Christian ascetic life. These loose monastic societies had some very important female voices who we can still read today. Theodora of Alexandria, Melania the Elder, and Amma Syncletica of Alexandria are all woman of the early Christian period who deliberately chose an ascetic monastic life in the desert and who can provide inspiration and joy to women today, especially among those who look for feminine inspiration in monasticism.

Out of the Egyptian desert, a figure rose who inspired thousands of monks who came after him, including those in the Celtic monastic tradition. St Anthony of Egypt is often called the father of Christian monasticism and his spiritual life is one of strict will and great heroism. His hagiography, Athanasius' Life of Anthony, was popular in the late Classical and early medieval world.

In this way, Classical cosmopolitanism lays groundwork for Christian monastic tradition writ large and for Celtic monasticism in particular. The border crossing nature of Rome, the Roman road, and Christianity came together and created a far reaching, powerful practice, pulling from the far corners of the Roman Empire and beyond. These boundary-breaking, spirit-changing cultural antecedents should be heeded by modern polytheist monastics.

Several Orthodox Christian sources have noted that Celtic monasticism is far more closely related to the ascetic practices of Byzantine (Orthodox) and Coptic monasticism than it is to Latin and Northern European monasticism, such as that practiced by St Benedict or the later St Francis of Assisi, with whom a standard American audience may be more familiar.

These kinships appear not in superficial practice, as Celtic monasteries never followed the rule of Basil of Caesurea, but in essence and in shared qualities. There is strong suggestion that some Celtic monks visited their brethren in the deserts of Egypt and they certainly exchanged texts, beliefs, and practices. There are, too, similarities between the Rule of St Columba and the Rule of St Basil which suggest conversation and shared inspiration.

This is not to say that Celtic monasticism is not without its own independent character and culture. It absolutely does and it is a character that is changeable from country to country and practice to practice. The monks who kept liturgical hours and created beautiful illuminated manuscripts in the monastery at Lindisfarne, acting as a beacon of light to all of Celtic Christianity, led very different lives when we compare them to the isolated hermits in the colchan in Fahan, County Kerry. Even the Rule of St Columba, which will be noted in detail later, is remarkably different from the later, broadly accepted Latin Rule of St Benedict, instituted and practiced through medieval Europe.

It is important to note here that we, as modern practitioners of a modern faith, are not the only people who view these early monks and nuns as the cultural inheritors of druidry and their indigenous, pagan, polytheistic past. The monks and nuns themselves accepted and understood this. This was a cultural and religious transformation, but they were still the same people they were before conversion. St Columba, that radiant monk of Celtic Christianity, famously declared, "Jesus Christ is my druid."

Many of the isles where Celtic monks formed their societies and communities, which were often cohabitational, much as the pre-Christian druids were a class that accepted women and men into their ranks, were traditional druidic islands. Iona, a Christian sanctuary unto the modern era, is known in Gaelic as Innis-nam Druidbneach or the Island of the Druids. Even the poetic metaphors wherein Celtic monks and nuns were referred to a bees can be seen as a continuation of the same correspondence between the druidic classes and honey bees.

This being said, we should not and cannot assume a direct correspondence between a Celtic Christian monasticism and whatever form of spiritual asceticism existed in the pre-conversion, multi-cultural world of the classical Celts. However, by understanding that Celtic monks came from the same culture that, at one time, understood and worshipped the same Powers and Spirits that call us today, we can safely draw inspiration and understanding. After all, it is through their continued devotion, despite conversion, to those self same Powers and Spirits, that we still have those stories to read, re-tell, and celebrate today. Through their shifting understanding of their world and Otherworld, so too can we reorient the same understanding to match our current, evolving cosmology of our world and the Otherworld.

Further discussion of a modern cosmology, relational to both the beliefs of pre-conversion Celtic ascetics and Celtic Christian monks will be reserved for a later section of this text. Comprehending cosmology is important to both the modern lay polytheist as well as the priest or ascetic with our traditions, but we must preface that with a thorough grounding in the history before we are equipped to fully explore that topic. The rise of the second Celtic Golden Age, accompanied by the monastic Age of Saints, is where many modern practitioners, Christian or polytheist, draw our understanding of ancient Celtic culture, but we should not limit it there. We must also look at how and why Celtic monasticism ceded to the Latin Rite.

The Celtic Christian Church, such as it existed until the Latin Rite took complete power by the 12th century, did not have the church, chapel, or cathedral that we modern religionists so closely associate with the Christian faith. Instead of organizing the holy orders and laity by parish or church, they were organized by abbey or monastery and the abbot or abbess of the institution would function somewhat like a bishop. In this manner, the countryside was peppered with a series of monastic societies that served the people in a considerably different manner than our modern conception of a priest with a parish.

These monastic institutions were not inherently sex-segregated. According to some sources, the famous abbey at Kildare, founded by St Brigid of Kildare, was one where, for a time at least, genders cohabitated and shared in a spiritual, ascetic life that might shock the more puritanical monastics today. As a queer practitioner myself, I find this inspiring and more than an historical footnote, just as many have found joy in the continuation of the veneration of Brigid as an Irish saint. This directly reveals, to me, that there have been other historic ways to view religious asceticism other than sex segregation and control.

As modern polytheists, who often function within animist cosmologies, we should note an important "heresy" among the Celtic Christian tradition, related to the Pelegian heresy I noted above. (The Pelegian heresy, a thorn in the side of the early medieval church, essentially held that human nature is inherently good.) The concept of original sin and the related theological idea of a sinful state of creation, often embraced by modern Christian churches, was not one universally embraced by the Celtic Christian monastic tradition. Even when individuals did agree with these theological tenets, they were up for debate and many religious leaders openly rejected it. In this way, we can embrace a specific Christian heritage that often openly recognized the inherent worth and holiness of this world as well as the Otherworld.

Within these monastic institutions, they most likely followed some kind of office of hours or a rule. However many of those used during the rise of the second Celtic Golden Age have been lost to time or the plunder of Ireland, first by the Vikings and then by the English. A rule in the monastic sense, such as the Rule of St Columba or the Rule of St Benedict (sometimes called the Benedictine Rule), is the guideline of spiritual asceticism and general conduct that the members of a monastic tradition are expected to follow. The office of the hours is how a particular monastic order outlines their daily prayers. A typical period Latin office of the hours would be Matins (midnight prayer), Lauds (dawn prayer), Prime (early morning prayer), Terce (mid-morning prayer), Sext (midday or noon prayer), None (afternoon prayer), Vespers (evening prayer), and Compline (night prayer).

Happily, we do have access to the Rule of St Columba, a monk who, along with his followers, converted Scotland and much of northern England to their particular form of Celtic Christianity. His rule varies considerably from the Rule of St Benedict, if only in length. (The Rule of St Columba, as provided online by Fordham University is a single page. The Rule of St Benedict is a complete book). While attributed to St Columba, this rule, written down after his death, was probably not written by the man himself, however it does show the spirit of Celtic Christianity and Irish monasticism, in particular.

Notably, one of the rules laid down in this text is "Three labours in the day, viz. prayers, work, and reading." This is a very important part of Irish monasticism. While it may be a stretch to say that the Irish saved civilization, as has been posited by Irish-American historian Thomas Cahill, Irish and Irish-derived monasteries were vitally important centers of learning, who preserved knowledge and produced saints, bards, and intellectuals, as the rest of Europe plunged into the Dark Ages after the fall of Rome.

The fall of the Western Roman Empire was a complex social, political, and economic disaster. As Rome retreated from its furthest imperial holdings, first in Britain, but then in Gaul and Iberia, those regions fell into chaos. The Plagues of Justinian – mysterious, fast moving, catastrophic diseases that moved from the fertile Nile valley as far north as Scotland and Scandinavia in a matter of years – further destroyed the social stability in regions who had been dependent on Roman power to provide that. Without protection from Roman soldiers, they were vulnerable to marauding tribes and thieves. Without the oversight of Roman government and access to Roman taxes, their roads, access clean drinking water, and other governmental infrastructure crumbled. Certainly, the city of Rome itself, overwhelmed by invasion and collapsing in on itself, could not provide support during the best of times, much less when a plague that rivals the Bubonic Plague in scope ravaged the countryside. Many thought it was the end times and, for the many who did die, it was.

Celtic Christianity, and monasticism in particular, existed, to a degree, outside of this frightening and, frankly, dire end of civilization. With monastic centers of learning in Iona, Kildare, and Lindisfarne, they were safe from the slow, chaotic death of the Western Roman Empire. They had never been Roman and never depended on imperial Rome to structure their world. As the people of the European countryside scattered to far villas and began to develop individualized feudal structures that would politically define the early Middle Ages, Irish monks and nuns read, prayed, and worked.

This literacy, in Latin and their native Celtic tongues, helped to preserve information, culture, and religion that may have otherwise been lost in the disorder, bloodshed, and turmoil inherent in the end of a civilization as ancient and vast as imperial Rome. The scribes laboriously copied out Gospels and full Bibles in an era when the Bible had not yet been codified and the printing press was nearly a thousand years from being invented. They also wrote down their own folklore, cultural stories, and myths of their own gods. Ascetics in Ireland took the time to write out the Book of Invasions, giving us a glimpse of their own view of the creation and history of their homeland. They did not attempt to unify these stories over time or region, but have left us a legacy that we still work to understand.

Thus, from this information, modern interpreter of this ancient institution can understand values and practices important to the Celtic monastic tradition that we can later bring into our own daily and annual practices. Erudition is a value the Celtic monks held dearly. While not single handedly, they preserved the knowledge of Europe from Christian and pre-Christian times until continental Europe was ready to flourish once again with the twelfth century renaissance. They also valued cultures and beliefs that went beyond their own. Just because they had chosen Christ did not mean that they fully abandoned the Dagda, the Boanne, or Aengus Og. They made the choice to remember Cuchulain and the Fianna and the Lands of Promise, which they still imagined as a form of Christian paradise.

They valued communal practices and exchange of ideas, even with those who are unlike themselves. As mentioned earlier, the Celtic monks were known to have visited the Coptic ascetics in the deserts of Egypt. Not only did they visit Egypt to learn and share what they had learned and their unique Celtic culture, they also brought back ideas about religious rule, art, society, and community structures. The choice to cross over what was increasingly becoming the line between the Occidental and Oriental may have eventually aided in Celtic Orientalization, but that value is one that we can carry forward today.

It has been posited, admittedly by Orthodox and Coptic sources, that the well known intricate art known as Celtic knotwork may, in fact, be the result of Coptic or Byzantine influence on the native Celtic artistic inclinations. Certainly, it does not appear in the historic record until the rise of Celtic monasticism. We can use this, if we so choose, as the vitally important visual cue to remind us of this particular value.

The Celtic tradition of peregrinatio, or the pilgrim voyage, took on a new importance as Britain and continental Europe receded from the light of Rome into the Dark Age. Many of the earlier stories, such as the famous one of St Brendan the Voyager, took to their coracles and were called to the Otherworld, with accounts of the lands beyond the Ninth

Wave or possibly the Americas or Greenland. Obviously, some undertook the arduous journey from the Celtic homelands to Coptic Egypt. However, as the Celtic monastic system came into its own during the second Golden Age and the Age of Saints, these voyages were increasingly to Britain and continental Europe, where they brought their own culture, education, and theologies with them.

According to tradition, the pilgrim, having experienced the spiritual call to leave their homeland or monastic center, to enter into a voluntary exile in order to better commune with the Holy, would sometimes cast even the direction and power over their journey to the Divine. They sometimes would ride boats at the open sea without rudder or oar, in order to allow their pilgrimage to be entirely directed (or ended) by Divine will alone. Although they did preach Christianity and educate others on their personal voyage of devotion, those were secondary characteristics or by products of their voluntary exile.

This yielding of self completely to the Divine – or, for an alternative view, the call of the Divine to give oneself in service and work – was known to early Irish and Celtic theologians and monastic practitioners as a form of "white martyrdom." Martyrdom, in our modern world and especially to neopagans, can have a bad reputation, so it's worth taking a quick moment of analysis. "Red martyrdom" is physical death for the faith. "Blue (or green) martyrdom" is the act of entering into the ascetic life, separated from the world, performing labor, and respecting taboo. "White martyrdom" is giving one's life to ascetic and spiritual practices and beliefs, giving up one's own direction for Divine will. This is a practice and thought form familiar to our communities.

It is commonly held among those seeking out a polytheistic monastic practice that many of us experience a very real spiritual calling from very real powers, spirits, and deities. Others in our community hold a kind of understanding that when a person acts on this or other callings – entering into the roles of spirit worker, shaman, priest/ess, nun, or monk – we are, in many ways, giving our life to the calling and those Who have called us. Sometimes these roles come with their own prohibition, taboo, or geas, whether from the role itself or one given by the Powers who call us. This is not unlike the ancient idea of white and green/blue martyrdom and, while it does not map on them perfectly, it can help bridge our understanding of these pilgrims and their wild, powerful yielding to the Holy.

With this, potentially greatest, act of white martyrdom, where the Celtic Christian monk found the internal will to place their life in the hands of the Divine, not just through asceticism but through Divinely ordained (and sometimes controlled) travel, they spread across Europe and, potentially, any where their little coracles and the will of the Holy could take them. With them they carried their own cultural understanding of the world, the teachings and values of Celtic Christianity, and the erudition of the monastery. They combined a fiercely heroic (and joyful) understanding of the world with education, asceticism, and a religiosity that echoes down to us more than a full millennium after they were absorbed into the Latin rite.

So how were they absorbed into that rite which still, today, dominates the Catholic Church? If the Celtic Christian monastic tradition offered an option that was different from the Latin rite, but lively, vital, and cherished, how was it that it died, only to be sought out again a thousand years later?

Although something so truly alive, something so ensouled, cannot truly die, Celtic Christianity did fall to the Roman Church.

While Celtic Christianity and the Latin rite, among other contemporary Christianities, were working together, to one degree or another, to bring Christianity to Europe (and beyond), they were also in fierce competition as to who was practicing Christianity in the correct way. In addition to different ecclesiastical structures, Celtic Christianity differed from the Latin rite in some ways that, at the time, were seen to make them fundamentally incompatible, including how measured the liturgical year, their understanding of baptism, the tonsure, and the liturgy.

The beginning of the clash between the Celtic Christian Church and Latin rite is hard to pin down, but it likely began before the Age of Saints and Second Celtic Golden Age. The strength of that cultural rising probably pushed back against the power of the Latin rite and Rome, but it was only so strong. As the Latin calendar and Benedictine Rule took a hold in southern Europe, they became a strong contender. Their central authority in the Vatican and the inheritance of the Pope offered, to some, an authority and stability they did not see in the idiosyncratic Celtic Christian monastic tradition.

Even though the Celtic lands were nominally Christian by the time imperial Rome collapsed upon its own weight, they were not the same kind of Christians as those in the Mediterranean. Indeed, they invented white and blue or green martyrdom because red martyrdom was unknown in Ireland. Certainly, by the time Pope Gregory sent Augustine of Canterbury to the British Isles, the monasteries at Iona and Lindisfarne were well established.

Over the next several hundred years, the island of Britain was an island experiencing spiritual and physical warfare on many sides. Even as both the Latin and Celtic church made a serious mission of converting both native peoples and invading Norse, Angles, Saxons, and Jutes, they also fought against one another. These inter-Christian battles often came to a head when municipal leader married a different kind of Christian and they had to choose a calendar by which to run the region and what kind of priest or monk to have as part of the royal household.

In theory, the Synod of Witby, around 663 CE, resolved the differences between the Celtic Christian church and the Latin rite. Of course, actual history is rarely as tidy as an entire religious culture ceding in one year to another. Celtic Christianity was no different. Various parts of Celtic Britain resisted the decisions made at the Synod at Witby for about two hundred years.

Ireland, with its distance across the Irish Sea and fiercely entrenched monastic system, resisted longer. It was only with St Malachi of Armagh and the Synod of Cashel in 1172 CE that all of Ireland finally came under the Latin rite. Notably, the Synod of Cashel was organized at the behest of Henry II of England, who arrived at Irish shores with his invading, colonizing Norman army the previous year.

With the Synod of Cashel, the soul of Celtic monasticism fell dormant for a very long time. Celtic lands were ravaged in the following centuries, at war or held as colonies by their enemies. However, it did not die. Perhaps, it spent a little time in the Otherworld, healing itself of the wounds its heart was experiencing.

The Celtic Revival beginning in the 17th century brought the Celtic spirit back into the light for those in power. Of course, the people of Celtic nations had never lost their spirit or their heart, but those in power had spent the previous six centuries attempting to destroy their traditions and would continue to do so. Many neopagans and modern polytheists are familiar with both the joys of Celtic Revival and some of the problems their perspectives.

As they were often French, Spanish, English, and Anglo folklorists and occultists, those who brought the Celtic cultures and spiritualities into the Western mind were also implicit in the colonization and suppression of those self-same cultures. However, much of our modern curiosity and desire for that soul, that spiritual tradition that carried the Celtic people on spiritual voyages with oarless coracles on the open sea, come out of that time. As inheritors of these traditions, we must maintain awareness of the problems and pains of our history.

I believe that today, in the early 21th century, we can embrace a new Celtic monastic tradition as modern polytheists. I say that, not as someone from Celtic lands, but as a member of the Irish Diaspora who lives with something like that far flung Celtic spirit. If we are deliberate, if we are thoughtful, and, above all, if we listen to those spirits and powers and shining ones who call to our hearts and souls, we can create for ourselves just as meaningful and powerful a new monastic tradition as they practiced 1500 years ago.

Shall I abandon the comforts and benefits of my life
Seeking the Lands of Promise my forefathers knew
Sail on the face of the depths where no riches or fame
or weapons can protect, where no one honors my name?
Shall I take leave of my friends and my family
And my beautiful native land,
With tears in my eyes
As my knees mark this final prayer in the sand?
Oh, Lords of Mystery, can I trust You on the sea?

Boann of the stars,
And Manannan of the ravenous waves,
I will hold fast my course
through the dangers I must brave.
Ladies of the mysteries, Your spirits will watch over me,
Lords of the mysteries, when I trust You on the sea.
(St Brendan's Mountain Prayer, adapted)

OUR CULTURAL
CHOICES

By invoking both the real history and ongoing living tradition of Celtic Christian monasticism and naming this a tradition of Celtic polytheistic monasticism, we are making an active decision to be a part of modern Celtic cultures. Some people reading this text may already be a part of a Celtic culture, such as those living in Ireland, Wales, Brittany, Scotland, the Isle of Man, Cornwall, and Galicia. Some of the people coming to this tradition are likely to be part of the Celtic diaspora, such as myself, a member of the extensive Irish diaspora in the United States. Others may be drawn to the cultural aspect of this practice because of their specific calling or because of an interest in a Celtic culture.

Religion - and make no mistake, this is a religious practice - is something that, when done well and right, changes a person's life. It is not a robe that one puts on to celebrate holidays and tend shrines and then hangs in the closet when going to work or raising children. Religion and culture go hand in hand because they deeply inform one another and co-create each other.

Religion and religious practice and spiritual beliefs infuse the minutiae of one's life. It may make the difference of pausing to give thanks over a meal. It will likely inform the values and rites parents or guardians pass on to their children. It may affect how a practitioner sees family and social structures. For the devotionalist or monastic practitioner, it will almost certain change how one structures their day, decorates their homes, observes the passage of time, and even where they live.

In this way, religion and culture are integral to one another. This is one reason that mainstream religionists, such as Protestant Christians in the United States, have, historically and in modern times, often panicked as the concept of the religious practice of a region changing. While xenophobia and bias are obvious and commonly cited reasons, the change of religious practice and spiritual belief create a directly observable change in culture and values as well. This can be disconcerting or upsetting for those who do not want to embrace such a change.

So by choosing to engage in a religious and spiritual practice informed by Celtic cultures, we are making a decision to embrace the values, morals, and core standards of those Celtic cultures as well as the practice of an ascetic devotionalism. This is something we must enter into with open eyes (and open hearts) before we directly explore the cosmology and practices of a new Celtic polytheistic monasticism. It is only by being honest, clear, and sincere in entering into this practice that any of us will be able to truly embrace it and commune with ourselves and with the Divine.

The Celtic cultures have held a peculiar position of fascination for occultists and neo-pagans since at least the eighteenth century, when Edward Williams - also known as Iolo Morganwg - began the Druid Revival. While the colonial, imperial powers of England, France, and Spain did what they could to destroy Celtic cultures and peoples, the occultists (and later, neo-pagans) were enamored by those self-same cultures and the people that were being degraded, impoverished, and killed by the dominant imperial nations. This push-pull of attempted destruction and spiritual allure has created something of a tension in the neo-pagan and polytheist communities that should be addressed.

The Celtic cultures are living cultures. They are primarily still held by the imperial nations that historically overwhelmed them. Even Ireland is still a divided nation and island. Wales and Scotland are recognized as nations within the United Kingdom, but lack both self-rule and full sovereignty. Cornwall is a county and the Isle of Man is a Crown dependency. Brittany is considered a cultural territory of France. Galician Celtic culture and literature are celebrated in that autonomous community in Spain and in Portugal.

(I am choosing deliberately to include Celtic Iberia here despite the fact that Galicia was rejected from the Celtic League on the basis of the loss of their indigenous language. As an American writer, I obviously have no control over the Celtic League's standards, only my own. However, Galicia has real and obvious Celtic heritage in which they take distinct pride and celebrate. I cannot, in my heart of hearts, reject that rich and abiding culture merely because Spain was more successful at eradicating their linguistic ties to their history and heritage than France and England were.)

They are living cultures and ones with which we can and must interact if we choose to embrace a Celtic spirituality. They were not eradicated by the imperial powers of Europe, despite their best efforts, and when we, as neo-pagans and polytheists, treat them as dead cultures which we can loot like corpses on a battlefield, we are rewarding England, France, and Spain for their colonial efforts. That is morally repugnant, aligning us with those people who created the Irish Potato Famine, enacted the Highland clearances, destroyed all viable records of Galician language, created internment camps for Breton separatists, used Wales as a testing ground for this new imperialism known as colonialism, and made Cornwall the poorest county in in the fifth wealthiest nation in the world.

While we often harp on the idea that we are not part of living traditions, such as those who have surviving folk religions, this is only partially true. When we say that, we do grave (colonial) disservice to the fact that these cultures, these nations, these peoples are still very much alive and, for the most part, still doing battle against imperial cultures that would much rather have them destroyed. England, France, and Spain would be collectively happier if the Celtic peoples subjected to their rule would give up on their differences - be that language, religion, literature, or any other cultural variance - and simply "become" truly English, French, or Spanish. When we call them dead because they converted to Christianity along with literally everyone else in Europe, we may be the ones killing them.

For those of us who are either already living in Celtic nations or who live in the diaspora, our families having been scattered by those imperial powers, connecting to a Celtic spirituality may be a way of embracing this living culture and powerful heritage of resistance. Those of us living outside of Celtic nations should be careful to consider how we fit into the dominant culture of our own nations, be that Canada, the United States, Australia, or any other nation, and how we are embracing a Celtic value and culture in our spiritual lives, as well as how that reflects in our daily living. Ongoing engagement with culture and values is, of course, an important part of any spiritual practice and we must always embrace this aspect.

For those without cultural ties to a living Celtic culture (and getting a genetic test and learning that one's familial heritage is 47% from the British Isles does not give anyone ties to a living culture), it may be worthwhile to take a moment of silence and consider why they are entering into a Celtic practice. There are many good reasons for someone without these native connections to want to enter into a Celtic polytheistic monastic practice, not the least of which is being called to monasticism by a Celtic Deity or Power. Others may have found a communion to the Divine through an aspect of a Celtic culture or while on vacation or pilgrimage in a Celtic nation. (El Camino de Santiago, which culminates in Galicia, is a powerful pilgrimage that has brought thousands, not all of whom are Roman Catholic, closer to communion with the Divine.)

There are other reasons, however, that are not so benign. We must remember, of course, that every Celtic nation has a long history of being subjected to colonial powers and suffering under imperial forces. As polytheists and neo-pagans, we must recognize the occultist and neo-pagan history of both treating these cultures as dead and merely raiding them for what we deem worthy. We also have an inheritance of respected people in our communities stating their beliefs or spiritual systems and slapping the words "Celtic," "Welsh," "Irish, or "Scottish" on the label because we know our books will sell better that way. This means that we, as polytheists and neo-pagans, must also recognize our history in the colonization of Celtic nations. We, too, have been part of the problem.

Thus, we all must reflect deeply upon ourselves and our own motivations. The desires of the ascetic and the drives of the imperialist are, after all, different. If we are coming to Celtic polytheistic monasticism because we desire monasticism and we believe that we can use Celtic culture to make that more appealing, dress it up in a way that makes it more alluring, or intend to raid the history of the culture but not interact with it's living peoples, we come at Celtic nations as colonizers and should abandon the task, if only for ethical reasons. If, on the other hand, we truly desire to embrace that culture, whichever nation and people we find ourselves among, and have that culture inform our practice, our ethics, and our lives, then we can move forward humbly and prepared to do the work.

Engaging in living Celtic cultures does not have to involve a great deal of money. I am not writing this text or proposing this practice as one only for those who have a great deal of free time and the disposable income to spend several weeks a year in living Celtic nations. If a particular practitioner or family or group of monastic practitioners have the time and money to do so, this may be a lovely way to become involved in the living culture, particularly if these trips can either be in the form of pilgrimage to holy sites or to the same village, where the practitioner(s) can become involved in cultural and daily life. It is an ideal of mine to be able to one day do that regularly.

However, this is probably an unrealistic immediate ideal for most practitioners, at least on a regular and ongoing basis. When we live oceans away from the living Celtic nations and are also engaged the sometimes monumental efforts of keeping body and soul together, such spiritual and cultural trips can seem beyond imagination. A pilgrimage, whether walking el Camino de Santiago in Galicia or visiting Kildare in Ireland or praying at the megalithic stones near Carnac in Brittany - can be a powerful act of faith. Ongoing community engagement in a living Celtic nation is, of course, a wonderful opportunity to give of oneself and engage in culture and life. However, these are not always options available to everyone.

There are, though, many ways to engage with living Celtic cultures, especially in this era of instant global communication. Several Celtic nations, Ireland in particular, have specific programs in order to engage emigrants and members of the diaspora throughout the world. Language has been long known to be important to Celtic cultures, to the point of excluding Galicia from the Celtic league, and learning the language of a nation is a unique way of engaging with its literacy and worldview. There, too, may be cultural clubs for emigrants and members of the diaspora. We can engage in traditional handicrafts and cooking, especially when we look forward to celebrating holidays and gatherings of friends and family.

So, too, can we engage in reading texts and works from members of the Celtic nations, rather than interpretations of their imperial overlords. This means, often, that we might look at the writings of the late nineteenth century Celtic Revival with a bit of a cynical eye, particularly when they are written by French or English authors. Certainly, for books written on colonized people by colonizers, we should always view their critiques (and their praise) with several large grains of salt and should not use them as be-all end-all definitions of those cultures they were exploiting and destroying.

We can also be honest about our shortfallings. None of us will ever meet some unrealistic platonic ideal of anti-colonial Celtic nationhood, particularly those of us who live outside of those nations (and for those who are living in Celtic nations, I encourage you to be kind to yourselves and recognize your colonial heritage). It's something to consider, but we cannot self-flagellate for failing to meet that. The future and our goals (cultural, spiritual, religious, familial, economic) will always move ahead of where we are now. To meet our goals is to stagnate and to fail. In moving forward, we must recognize that it is the motion, like the tide of the ocean, that compels us, not the shore.

This is what I mean that this text is about a Celtic polytheistic monastic practice. In the coming sections, I will break down what it means to be both polytheistic and monastic, but here is being Celtic. I strongly believe that, even outside of the physical regions publically recognized as Celtic, we can engage in Celtic culture and that this culture is separate and distinct from other cultures. If we are to do this, it will be an act that separates us from our contemporaries, but in a good and positive way and one that can, potentially, contribute to those living cultures with which we engage.

O Great and Mysterious Ones,
By whose grace we are called,
Grant us justice,
Grant us prudence,
Grant us strength;
Give us wisdom,
Give us trust,
Give us reconciliation;
Gift us faith,
Gift us love,
Gift us silence,
That our life may be enriched
And we might know your will,
Bless our communion now and forever.
(Prayer of St Hilda, adapted)

OUR UNDERSTANDING

As we move away from the history of classical Celtic Christian monasticism and toward a modern practice of polytheistic Celtic monasticism, it is vital that we take the time to redefine our cosmology and our needs. As a polytheistic, and often animistic, people, our belief in the spiritual substance of this world and the Otherworld are inherently different than that of the Celtic Christian monks during the Dark Ages. And, even if we could fully understand the cosmology and beliefs of the pre-conversion Celts, we are a modern people religious with modern needs in the 21st century and our cosmology must recognize that in order for us to function in it.

Particularly as some of us, potentially including you, kind reader, are contemplating or have already entered white or green/blue martyrdom, it is imperative that we have the ability to define, to some degree or another, the Powers and Spirits to which we offer ourselves. It would be dangerous, to say the least, to enter the oarless coracle without knowing to whom we have committed our faith. This can be difficult and complicated, but it is supremely worthwhile.

There will also always be a difference of opinion and belief, as our polytheistic faith is a folk faith in the true sense of the term. I do not pretend to be an authority on this topic, much less a final authority. I merely offer a potential cosmology and view of the spiritual world and Otherworld that allows for a monastic function. This is the way in which I see these worlds and the foundation of the practices set forth in this text.

Rather than define ourselves relationally to Christianity, which will forever center Christianity in how we define ourselves, I would rather the we, as Celtic polytheists and polytheistic ascetics, define ourselves. If we must be relational to someone, it should be with other neo-pagans and polytheists. Let us take pride in who we are and what we believe. Let us own that we are a true religious tradition in our own right.

If we are relational to other polytheist and neo-pagan belief systems or pantheons, it is in that Celtic powers exist more relationally and liminally than is commonly standard in many other systems. We do not understand Powers to have specific and proprietary dominions and functions. For example, while in the Hellenic pantheon we can look to Hera as a goddess presiding over marriage and Hades as having dominion over the dead, we cannot make such correspondences in much of the Celtic world.

To simply look at the realm of the dead, in a simplistic and Irish manner, we have the phrase, "entering the house of Donne," which is often used in mythological texts to indicate that someone has died. However, we have a wide variety of psychopomps other than Donne, the first Milesian to die. The Morrigan, in a variety of forms including the battle crow and Washer at the Ford, both predicts death and comes to harvest the soul. Mannanan mac Lir is the chieftain or king who presides over Otherworldly islands and lands which are often thought to be the place where the souls of the dead reside. Crom Cruach is relational to death, in ways that are somewhat unclear in the literature. Brigid and Airmid, as the creator of keening and mourner of her brother respectively, are also directly relational to death without being death deities. Yet none of these deities have a dominion in the same sense as the Mediterranean gods and all may be invoked for different practitioners who are experiencing different affinities to death.

Our Deities are not proprietary and intensely separate from one another. Just as the concept of the family or clan shared honor and responsibility, so, too, do our Gods and Powers share honor and responsibility. It is improper to suggest that only one Power can have dominion over an experience, a natural phenomena, or people. Just as Manannan and his whole household, including Fand and Cliodna, can be invoked when having a spiritual oceanic experience, so too can Nertha and Li Ban. For us, the goal, when seeking out these Powers, is not "To whom does this thing belong?" but, "Who is calling me with this experience?" And even with a group of people experiencing the same phenomena, different Powers may be calling different people.

Our deities and our spirits also experience a deep and abiding kinship with one another. While some traditions honor a separation between types of spirit and even type of deity, this does not appear to be true in the Celtic traditions. Again, I speak from a very Irish space, but this can be extrapolated as a generalized truth across the traditions.

Even as the Tuatha de Danaan and other deities retreated into the mounds and hills when the Milesians invaded Ireland, so, too, do the fairy folk and spirits come from the sacred mounds, raths, and trees of their people. So, too, do the goddesses of sovereignty, such as Sinnan or Eiru, Bonba, and Fodla , have strong relations to both the sovereign water, land, and sky spirits of all lands and to humanity, who own our own sovereign bodies. Our system of belief has a unique, deeply spiritual and profound interconnection and relation among the Deities, or High Powers; the Spirits, or Lesser Powers; the Humans, or ourselves; and the Holy Dead, who may or may not belong to any one or more of the previous sects.

These are all liminal, not intrinsic, categories. A spirit, being, or personage can belong to one, more, or none of these categories and still occupy a space of power of be ensouled. Some of our shining powers can also move into the spirit space. Some of our spirits move into the roles of deities or powers. And, still too, some of our holy dead can move into the faery or spirit space and back again.

So, too, is this why it is not just the Otherworld which is holy, but this world as well. The mounds, tombs, oceans, wells, rivers, and trees inhabited by our Gods and Powers are in this world and the Otherworld. We will join the dead at the end of our life and it is not death alone that sanctifies them. Our world is sacred and the Otherworld is sacred and they are as intertwined as a braid. The shift between one and the Other may be readily apparent or not, because we are simply moving from one holy space to another.

Because the spirits, Powers and Deities occupy shifting roles and share dominion over human experiences and the physical world itself, our experiences, as worshippers and as monastic practitioners, will inherently be personal and experiential. Many of us will have shared experiences, particularly if we serve and work with Deities and Shining Ones of ancient power, but not having that shared experience is in no way an indication that a person is doing something wrong. Each of us who has been called is called to do something different. Even if two are as alike as twins and called both to monastic practice by the same Great Power, their spiritual and religious path is unique and separate.

Our Gods, Powers, and spirits carry with them certain

elements of danger and this text would be remiss if we did not address that. They are powerful and They are Otherworldly and, because They can sometimes to appear to be worldly and like us, we can forget that. While our Powers have called us for a reason, we should still approach them with caution and awe. Even a lesser spirit, such as a puca or fear dearg, is an Otherworldly power and regarded as such Our Shining Ones often move among us and sometimes, in myths and folktales, it is not uncommon to unexpectedly come across a Power while travelling from rath to rath or the commute from home to work. The knowledge that these Powers can be encountered by chance – not merely when we enter a chapel or holy glade – heightens that sense of both accessibility and risk. They have Their own will and Their own directions. The stakes with our Otherworldly counterparts can be high, if only because we cannot guarantee shared motivation and goals. We need to respect that.

We can still encounter Them in this way in the contemporary world. Our Shining Ones are not trapped in the vellum pages of an illustrated manuscript nor are they bound to the primeval history of pre-conversion Celtic lands. Not only do They call to contemporary neo-pagans and polytheists in all parts of the world today, but our Powers and Spirits join us in the present-day. They call us to do work in our own world, with contemporary gifts and contemporary practices.

As much as we can draw on the history and tradition of the people who have gone before us, we have different physical, psychological, and spiritual needs than the people who worshipped the Tuatha de Danaan and their contemporaries before the Common Era. The world our ancestors inhabited is one so functionally different from the one in which we live and labor and worship that we cannot recreate it in an effort to somehow create an "authentic" experience for our Powers and Shining Ones. And They know that. Knowing that, They do not want to us to do recreate the past, but to create a new, living future.

Our modern needs and modern spaces allow for our liminal and expansive Deities and Powers to occupy new spaces and meet new needs. They are not frozen in Iron Age Ireland or pre-Roman Gaul any more than we, as people, are trapped there. The spiritual and religious needs of our daily lives have changed and our Gods are prepared to meet us where we are. We can and should, of course, learn from the myths and folklore of the medieval period as well as the folklore of the 19th century, but that is not where the story of our Shining Ones ends. We worship and engage with living powers. They were not called the Undying Ones for nothing.

An example of a great and ancient power moving into the modern world is the Morrigan, who have their own modern priests and priestesses. In medieval manuscripts, she is a tripart (or more) goddess of war, sovereignty, and death, among other aspects. She, along with a few other Great Powers such as Manannan mac Lir, pre-dates the arrival of the Tuatha de Danaan in Ireland. She often acts in specific roles, when functioning as the Morrigan and not the individual Goddesses who make up the Great Queen, as can be seen in the Tain Bo Cuailnge, where she and Cuchulain go back and forth unto his death.

She (or They) have adapted well to our fast paced, multicultural, contemporary world and the very modern needs of Her worshippers. I am not devoted to her, nor have I taken any priestly oaths, but I have personally seen Her act as a holy agent of personal sovereignty, stepping in when people have had their personal power and autonomy, especially bodily autonomy, taken from them. In this way, She can and does act as an Otherworldly tripart agent of restorative justice.

All of our Gods and Powers have adapted in this way to our contemporary experiences and needs. They understand that we live in a post-industrial world, one where we are interconnected and codependent on one another in incredibly complex ways. They understand that many of our cultural values have changed and transformed over time. They know that our languages have changed – and that many of us, at least in the beginning, will call on them in our native tongues and not Theirs. (Although it can be an act of political resistence and spiritual act of asceticism to learn a language They knew before, They still understand us when we pray in modern dialects of English.)

They also understand that we have modern, contemporary values that reflect, not just the faith and Otherworld that we have, but our culturally-bound understanding of the world. Sometimes, as with sovereignty, we are called to a deeper, broader, more modern expansive understanding of the value, one writ large to include a nation's sovereign right to rule itself but also a person's sovereign right to bodily autonomy. As such there are several important groups whose value is often called into question by modern society who are affirmed within this religio-spiritual context.

Women have long had a tradition of leading monastic practices in the context of the Celtic monastic tradition. Abbesses led orders of men and women as skillfully and as openly as abbots in Celtic Christianity. Looking to the distant past, we know that there, too, was a tradition of female druids working and practicing in the same context as male druids. From Fidelma to St Brigid of Kildare, these are not nameless women, but powerful druids, nuns, abbesses, saints, and even Deities. There is no reason, whether cultural, historical, or religious that a woman, of any kind, should barred from monastic practice on the basis of her womanhood.

So, too, are there customs, both in the pre-conversion Celtic world and in the Celtic Christian tradition, of queer figures featuring prominently in Celtic life. Of course, queer is an anachronistic term, a modern Victorian category we can cautiously apply to history, but it is the best I can do with limited space. From the Roman's fearful accounts of an egalitarian queerness among Celtic soldiers in Gaul to Cuchulain's eternally beardless face, heroes and soldiers were very capable of defying our modern categories of normative sexuality and gender. There is the medieval tale of an Irishwoman impregnated, accidentally, by her married lover, so that she came to accidentally carry her lover's husband's child. Here and with the relationship between Brigid and Darlughdagh, holy women, too, could exist outside of our modern conventional categories of gender and sexuality while maintaining their roles. So, too, should these not pose any barrier, in and of themselves, to monastic practice.

If we draw on pre-conversion and Celtic Christian historical sources, as well as our modern, secularly-informed values, we will see that race, ethnicity, heritage, and skin color are in no way barriers to either being called by the Powers of the Celtic Otherworld or practicing devotional asceticism in a Celtic monastic tradition. The pre-conversion Celts were a massive, multicultural tribal peoples who travelled, we suspect, from the Indian subcontinent to the far reaches of Britain and Ireland. Though ferocious in battle, the Celtic tribes, to our knowledge, did not engage in the kind of imperialism associated with some Greek city states and, later, Rome. Additionally, like many ethnic and national groups of the Classical period, they appear to have engaged in trade, communication, and fraternization with the many other ethnic and tribal groups surrounding them. The Celtic Christian tradition is fundamentally clear, with their contact with Coptic and Byzantine monastic traditions that cultural, political, and social barriers were not, in fact, barriers to sharing spirituality and monastic life. We would do well to imitate these forebears in this regard and, while we recognize that these barriers are very real in the modern world, they in no way bar a person from either monastic calling or monastic practice.

Many people who are called by the Spirits and Powers experience a disability of one kind or another. According to United States census data, roughly 1 in 5, or 20%, of the population of the United States self-report as living with a disability. That is roughly 56.7 million people, or more than the number of people living in California, our most populous states. It is just under twice the population of Texas, our second most populous state. Every practice and religious or secular organization should anticipate that members of this population will be among their members. Indeed, given the nature of disability, some previously able bodied members may become disabled during the course of their monastic practice.

More deeply, however, both in historic practice and in some

modern pagan practices, sometimes people with a disability or a chronic illness can consider that disability, illness, or difference as a part of their calling from the Shining Ones. This is obviously not true of everyone with a disability (nor does it mean that someone who is healthy cannot experience a calling). However, this aspect can be an important one, where the struggle with one's health can be refrained and better understood with a spiritual lens, is one that we can embrace, should a monastic practitioner experience that as right and true for themselves.

Certainly any of the monastic and ascetic practices in this text can be adapted and used by those with and without disabilities. For any of us with disability, I encourage you to start with where you are at right now. Certainly, the office of the hours often faces no barriers except time and spoons. It need not even be spoken aloud, should that pose an issue for a practitioner. Anyone, regardless of disability status, should work at developing their own monastic practice at their own pace, but disability status should not, in any case, bar someone from monastic calling or practice if they take it on for themselves.

Finally, we value discernment. Living, as we do, in a deeply spiritual and spirit-filled world, one where there are many paths one can choose to follow and one may be Called to follow, it can be a Gordian knot to understand what we are meant to do in this life. Sometimes a path looks right until we are many steps down it and we realize, quite suddenly, that this is not where we are meant to be. Especially in the pagan realm, it is not uncommon for a seeker to follow many different paths and faiths before finding the one that fits. For some, too, spirituality is a fluid thing and it is best for those people to follow different paths as they are so called.

In this case, if anyone reading this book feels the call to a polytheistic Celtic monastic practice, I invite you to try out the prayers, ascetic practices, and even the rule that follow in the rest of this text. However, I encourage anyone using this to practice discernment. Does this practice fulfill your calling? Is this something that is spiritually and devotionally fulfilling? Are you practicing it in a sustainable way, that energizes your spiritual life and connects you to your Gods and Powers?

This is my personal household practice. It does provide all of these things to me. I write this because I suspect it may provide these things to others as well and because there are not as many resources available as I would like. I built this out myself, working with my Gods and Shining Ones, and continue to build and adapt it. I encourage any and everyone who uses it to do the same.

Leave me alone with the holy as much can be.
As the tide draws the waters close upon the shore,
Make me an island, set apart,
Alone with the Gods and Powers, sained to You.
Then with the turning of the tide,
Prepare me to carry Your messages to the busy world
beyond,
The world that rush upon as a tide,
Til the waters come again and fold me back to you.
(Prayer of St Aidan of Lindisfarne, adapted)

OUR SPIRITUAL
ecology

The spiritual world we inhabit has an ecology and measured balance as much as the natural world does, and just as with the ecology of the natural world, we are an integral part of it and do not directly control it, despite the propaganda of the dominant, secular culture. The spirits of the land, sea, and sky; the souls of the Holy Dead; the Powers, spirits, and Deities make up the other players in this circular Great Dance that moves in and out of this world and the Otherworld. These powers (and we) interact with one another, some giving and some taking, in an eternal dance that works best when everyone knows their part and plays it well.

A calling to monasticism and monastic practice is a calling to a particular role, or set of roles, in this dance. It is one that may overlap with other roles and callings - that of the spirit worker, the shaman, the priest or priestess, the devotee, the teacher, the student, the hermit, the writer, the spiritual counselor, the mystic, the mendicant, the warrior - but it is also distinct from those roles. When we identify what the Powers call us to do - in this case, initiate a monastic practice - it helps clarify where we stand in the ecology of our spiritual world. By initiating prayer and asceticism, deliberately and with purpose, we begin to fulfill our spiritual roles and dance our rightful steps in this Great Dance.

Monasticism is the ascetic, often mystical and transcendental, side of the priestly ordained class of a religious faith. Even private vows, especially when combined with a public practice of prayers and asceticism, can function as a form of ordination by spirit. Certainly, ordination by spirit has a history within Celtic mythology and Celtic monastic tradition. Entering into a specific aspect of ordination, where the life of the devotee is given unto the Powers and Gods, is different than the priest, who may be giving his spiritual life directly to the community he or she serves.

In Celtic Christianity, as demonstrated previously, the monastic holy orders were the only priestly class , with monasteries functioning as religious centers and schools, foci of the social and ecclesiastical world, and with abbots and abbesses wielding the worldly power the late Classical and early medieval world accorded to bishops. This meant that, in addition to being monks and nuns committed to prayer and asceticism and, often, performing sacramental and liturgical rites, they were often also teachers, community organizers, political leaders, and official record keepers.

This does not mean that every individual called to a personal monastic practice is also called to take on students, lead group rituals, or engage in political activism. There are some who experience a call to a simple eremitic practice and some who are called to a stronger practice of asceticism through rigorous prayer and devotion. Monasticism, especially with a Celtic tradition, simply encompasses a much larger fold than that, one with many overlapping roles.

Some of these roles may come and go, moving like the tides on the shore. There are many stories from the days or early writing in Celtic lands of the hermit, safe in his colcan or island, who found himself suddenly, unexpectedly surrounded by students because his role and calling had shifted. Thus, we should be fully prepared for fluidity in our role or roles in this ecology of spirituality.

Discerning our calling and role is the first step and should be a meditation and prayer by which we can regularly take measure of our lives and part in the Great Dance. Our roles in the world shift and change because the needs of others - of other people, of spirits, of the Gods themselves, and even our own needs - change and fluctuate over time. As people spiritually engaged with something greater than ourselves - and, in the end, bigger than one single Power or Deity - we must constantly discern and distinguish where we are now and how to get where we need to go next.

An integral part of discernment is having a holistic understanding of what exactly our spiritual ecological system looks like. This is related to our Divine cosmology, in that our individualized personally active Spirits and Deities are an integral part of this system and it is They who organize the major steps and changes in this beautiful, eternal dance. However, it goes deeper and broader than simply our relationship to Those who have called us into a role of monasticism today and, actually, involves every soul and spirit we touch or even who can be touched.

In this sense, there is an ecology here of cooperative animism. Because of the eternity of the Otherworld, which is demonstrated not just in the literature from the twelfth century onward through the twenty-first, but even in how we refer to those citizens native to the Otherworld, the animism is inherently cooperative because we are in an eternal circle or spiral of life and death, but one that is shared. When we call the Great Powers, the Undying Ones, as we do even in the ogham kennings, as with Úr which is the "shroud of the undying one" in Bríatharogam Con Culainn, we recognize the perpetual cooperation and the timelessness of the Otherworld.

As monastic practitioners, in particular, we should be

humble enough to recognize that, in this undying ecosystem of shared spirits and souls between worlds, we are neither the most important nor the most interesting dancers in this Great Dance. We are important enough that we have been specifically and individually called, because our Powers and spirits are great but also deeply personal. Bride, for example, is a great and ancient Power, one who survived the crashing wave of Christian conversion and who came again to great prominence in our own time, but none of this prevents Her from also coming to us individually, with healing, inspiration, joy, companionship, and even private callings.

Importance to a singular Great Power, or even group of Powers, depending on one's calling and interpretation of the One(s) performing the calling, does not necessarily make a monastic practitioner more important or better (or more interesting) than anyone else in this diverse spiritual ecosystem. There is no particular reason that a person or persons who are of particular individual importance or regard to Scathach or Miach would be of interest to anyone else. Otherwise, the budding polytheist who themselves called by Ogma to academic work and skill in their youth would suddenly find themselves under the watchful eyes and scrutiny of far more than we currently expect or understanding in our modern milieu of historically grounded Celtic polytheism.

While it is not uncommon of a modern Celtic polytheist to find themselves close to, or working with, several Deities and Powers and perhaps aligning themselves with more than a couple spirits of land, sea, and sky, I have not personally encountered anyone who experienced the above hypothetical scenario. Generally speaking, I experience the Powers to have their own agendas, independent plans, and personal modus operandi, completely mysterious and unknowable to someone of my simple standing. It is also not my place to know why They act in the way they do. It is my place to fulfill my role in this Great Dance and to understand my life and my calling, which, honestly, is a lifetime's worth of work unto itself.

While I do not often question the reality of having a spiritual calling, I profess to have no idea why, in particular, I received that calling. I am not a special individual and I certainly have not experienced the intense interest, benign or malicious, of Anyone else, large or small. This suggests, to me, that the above assessment of myself as someone primarily uninteresting and unimportant is at least somewhat accurate.

Given my personal experience in the world, I suspect this is generally true of most people. While we are the heroes of our own life story and the directors of our own hero's journey, most other people and spirits do not give us the same honor in their own lives.

I have encountered people in the milieu of Celtic polytheism who have moved from Great Power to Great Power in a series of working relationships or unoathed devotions, I have not honestly experienced anyone who was either under the aegis of all Great and small spirits and Power nor anyone who was under inspection from those spirits altogether and assailed from all sides. The relationships in Celtic polytheism, both traditionally and in my modern experience, are generally cooperative and when they become negative or malign, it is due to a broken taboo or unintentional (or intentional) offense. This was not a worldview that traditionally believed the spiritual world to be a boot on the neck of the people.

In my personal experience, most spirits, from the Great Powers to the highly localized land spirit, are intensely interested in just doing what they need to do, much as people are. Most of the time, the life and work of a spirit is only tangentially related to me or any other human action or spiritual practice. The land spirit is acting upon the business of a land spirit and will likely be happiest if it can do that unimpeded. It is only when we, as humans, interfere with that course of action, whether spiritually through improper action or through physical acts of despoiling its body, such as dumping waste in its domain, that we can raise the ire of a spirit. Otherwise, it has no reason to be interested in direct action, benevolent or malicious, toward us or our society. This, too, is one of the reasons that right action and proper tribute is required for the blessing and sanction from a spirit, especially those of land, sea, and sky, who may be less interested in us that the Great Powers.

For this reason, I encourage the path of prayer and right action toward the spiritual world and the spiritual ecosystem of cooperative animism. Right action includes making offerings and appropriate communication, while also respecting taboo or geas. It means that we recognize that our daily actions are a part of our spiritual life and world and that everything and everyone affects everyone and everything. In the Celtic cosmology and worldview, while Otherworldly spirits certainly carry a level of danger, it is because they are Otherworldly and have their own agendas and rules, which are, by their very nature, not the agendas and rules of human society. These spirits and Powers are not seeking to harm people or societies, not without first having been riled or hurt by those same people or societies. It can be easy to cause unwitting offense, which is why it is so key to follow a path of right action, whether one is a monastic practitioner or not. I also suspect those who experience a calling to monastic or devotional practice may be held to a higher standard of action and deference, if only because we already interact, on a regular basis, with Otherworldly powers.

The ecosystem of our spiritual world mirrors natural ecology in that it shifts and changes over the course of the year. Many neopagan traditions reflect these seasonal traditions through their rituals mirroring that ecology. Whether this is lighting the Yulelog on the longest night of the year, to call back the sun, as they did in some Anglo-Saxon traditions or the Manx who celebrated a time between midsummer and St John's Night by paying the rent to their ancient king and landlord, we all understand, on one level or another, that different times of year can call for different ceremonies and prayers.

It would be inappropriate to celebrate Imbolc at Mabon, to use the modern Wiccan terms. This is also why people in the Southern Hemisphere are encouraged to use the holidays that follow their seasons, rather than the months of the year. Thus, Imbolc is always celebrated at early spring and Mabon at the autumnal equinox, even in a part of the world where lambing season may begin as early (or as late) as the turning of August.

Even times that may, on the surface, be similar, such as the so-called "thinning of the veil" that occurs at Samhain and Beltane, ought to be treated differently if the spiritual ecology is different. Just as the fall equinox and spring equinox are both times when day and night are perfectly balance, yet they herald different changes in seasons, so too do holidays signal changes for our spiritual ecosystem. We should heed these changes and follow them, much as we follow the literal ecological changes of the seasons. Even the most insulated urbanite pulls out sweaters and boots at the signs of cold weather and prepares for swimming season when the sun returns.

We take more time and effort, however, as monastic practitioners, to head the ecosystem of spirits around us, whether it means that we are following seasonal spiritual changes or discerning messages from the Powers or heeding the needs of a specific spirit. This is often a matter of quiet, silence, and sensitive judgment. As monastic practitioners, we do not only take action, we also wait, listen, and heed the needs of our community. Our community is much greater than merely those who share in our monastic practice.

This wider understanding of our community both has strong roots in Celtic Christian monastic practice and in wider modern neo-pagan and polytheistic belief systems. The syncretism of the two allows the modern monastic practitioner a world community to whom we can provide service and who we can see, in turn, as allies. Indeed, if the world is a community we can serve, for whom we can pray and hold silence, who can find refuge in our practice, then our practice has become a true monasticism.

Celtic Christianity, generally speaking, resists the gnostic concept of the Demiurge who has subjugated and damned the world, in opposition to the Supreme Being who awaits in a non-physical spiritually purified paradise. The gnostic division is one of dark, dangerous, bad, earthly, and bodily, against light, sacred, good, heavenly, and spiritual. Historically and modernly, Celtic Christians have embraced the holiness of the world and the sacredness of the physical.

This is one of the reasons they took themselves to the desert of the ocean and the purpose they undertook in bringing knowledge back to mainland Europe during the second Celtic Golden Age. This same pantheism is visible today in modern branches of Celtic Christianity.

May modern neo-pagans and polytheists have adopted an animistic understanding of the world(s), even those who have been called to very different deities and cultural worldviews. For those who have looked more deeply into the folklore and folk beliefs of the Celtic nations, particularly those with a robust and accessible folklore such as Ireland, Scotland, and Wales, we have often discovered that this general animism is supported by the spirits who have called us to these cultures, whether they are native or adopted. (Those who have been called to an adopted cultural understanding should, of course, be carefully respectful when learning about this calling and the spirits in that culture.)

When we combine these concepts, we reach a mutual understanding that the world, and everything in it, is sacred and holy. This does not mean that there are not sacred places, such as groves or chapels, or that some spirits, such as Deities, are not more holy or powerful. It means that everything has a spirit and every spirit is important, sacred, and worthy.

We cannot say that we have dominion over the world because we are the best. We are not. We cannot say that we have the right to destroy. We do not. We must say that we will use our gifts to the best of our abilities.

We must approach them with a humbleness that comes from awe and not from shame, because we, too, are a part of the world. If the world has a spirit and the physical can be elevated to the sacred, then we have a spirit and our bodies, too, can be elevated to the sacred.

In the end, this is the heart of our spiritual ecology. We cannot be a people merely waiting to shed our bones and the trials of this world, to enter into the sacred Summerlands and Isles of Apples and Woman as pure beings of light. We reject the idea of the Demiurge who has somehow stolen the world from us. This we reject wholeheartedly.

We will be and are a people who are a part of this world, who know how to bring out the Otherworld in this one, who know how to kindle the fire of the sacred in the centers of cities and hearths of rural homes, one at a time. We are a monastic people who, instead of retreating to the cloister, move in the world, interacting with people, spirits, and Powers as we are called. We understand them, we can discern their messages, and we can honor Them and They can honor us, just as They have honored us by calling us to this practice.

For those who are also called to other roles, such as the priest/ess, the teacher, or the spirit worker, it is important to balance the role and dance of being a monastic practitioner along with those roles. As many of us will have many social roles, such as a parent, an employee, or a spouse, we will also have to balance those dances and those responsibilities with that of being a monastic practitioner. There are other roles, too, such as that as a disabled person or that of being a public figure which require special considerations. None of these are incompatible with this worldview or this practice, but each person must take special consideration of their own dance and their own steps.

Those who occupy liminal, oppressed spaces will also find themselves with difference and specific steps in this Great Dance. Whether that is because we are disabled, queer, people of color in a colorist colonial world, women, lower class, or any other class that experiences an axis of oppression, we will experience specific difficulties. These difficulties do not arise from our monastic practice or from the Otherworld, but it can be through our practice that we can find a safe haven. Our steps as queer people or women or lower class people will be different and how we engage in our practice will differ, but these are variances to embrace. Our practices are because we are who we are and we are called as we are.

A significant part of my understanding of our spiritual ecosystems, as a queer disabled person myself, is that we are very distinctly called to our practices and actions as we are. Our callings do not demand us to become rich or white or able bodied or straight or any other personal aspect of the dominant paradigm of our prevailing culture. In fact, we may be especially called, in part, because we do not meet the requirements of that culture. Keeping that in mind, we should embrace those aspects of ourselves that are rejected by the world around us because they may be why we stand in this space today.

I arise today
Through the strength of the love of the spirits,
In accordance with land, sea, and sky,,
In service of Great Powers,
In the hope of the silver Branch of Glory,
In the prayers of mighty dead,
In lessons of those gone before us,
In faiths of the sages,
In innocence of children,
In deeds of the righteous.

I arise today
Through the strength of the world;
Light of the sun,
Splendor of fire,
Speed of lightning,
Swiftness of the wind,
Depth of the sea,
Stability of the earth,
Firmness of the rock.

I arise today
With the strength to pilot me;
With the might to uphold me,
With the wisdom to guide me,
With the eye to look before me,
With the ear to hear me,
With the word to speak for me,
With the hand to guard me,
With the way to lie before me,
With the shield to protect me,
With the hosts to save me
From snares of turmoil,
From temptations of wrong action,
From every one who desires me ill,
Afar and anear,
Alone or in a multitude.
(the Deer's Cry, adapted)

OUR RULE

A Rule of Polytheistic Celtic Monasticism
(adapted from the Rule of St Columba, attributed)

Be alone in a separate place. Leave from the city and the crowd if you cannot be common with the crowd.
Be always honest and open with the Shining Powers .
Have a secure place, with a door, that can be your enclosure.
Have a few religious friends to converse of the Shining Ones; to meet on holy days; to strengthen your connection with the holy and discuss your spiritual life.
Bless the idler and the gossip, but do not enjoin with them.
Yield yourself to devotional practice.
Be fortified and steadfast for white martyrdom.
Be fortified and steadfast for green martyrdom.
Constantly pray.
Have zeal in singing the office for the dead, as if every member of the dead was a particular friend.
Be constant in your vigils, from eve to eve.
Three daily labors: prayer, work, and reading.
Work divided into three parts: your own and the work of your place; secondly, your share of the work of your people; lastly, to help the neighbors, as by instruction, or writing, or sewing, or whatever labor they need.
Always strive.
Eat only when hungry.
Sleep only when tired.
Speak not except deliberately.
Be true in your devotion to the Gods, Powers, and spirits.
Be true in your devotion to the people.
The measure of prayer will be until tears come.
Or the measure of work of labor will be until tears come.
Or the measure of work of labor or of prayer will be until you sweat if tears are not free.

I believe this is a straightforward, self explanatory rule that, while ascetic and monastic in its guidelines, it is a labor of love and devotion. In the next section, I will go into detail about some of the specifics.

There are several rules from the medieval Rule of St Columba I deliberately removed and did not even attempt to adapt. They all have to do with the religious vows of poverty common to the Celtic Christian monastic tradition. According to their faith and culture, many monks and nuns would (and still will) give up their worldly wealth in order to enter into the white and green/blue martyrdom of the cell. It was, and is, a powerful statement of giving up worldly possessions and giving oneself up utterly to the Otherworldly powers Who call us.

However, in my day job, when I am not acting as a person religious, I work to help support people who are living near or below the poverty line. I know myself what it means to be poor in this time, this place, and this culture.

Maybe this is a concept that we can strive toward, as a broader community. However, the culture and infrastructure in place at places like Iona (founded 563 CE) and Lindisfarne (founded 635 CE) provided a very, very different definition of deliberate poverty than currently exists for monastic polytheistic neo-pagans. I cannot, in good conscience, recommend that anyone give up any kind of safety net they currently have - or may have future access to - in order to enter monastic practice.

I do not believe that our Gods and Powers want us to suffer in this way at the hands of our current system, if it is avoidable. I believe They call us for our service, not for that.

If you disagree with me, you are welcome to take a vow of poverty, but I cannot and will not ever ask for that.
I think there is a space where we can question the greed and the desire to build up wealth in this world, and that has a very valid place in monastic practice. We should not be accumulating things for the sake of saying that we have so many things: a big house to show that we can own more space than we can inhabit, expensive cars to show that we can be mindless about our travel, etc etc.

However, we live in a time where our ability to be fiscally conservative is intrinsically linked to our physical survival. I want anyone who takes on this path to live and live as best they can. My God wants me to live and be safe in His service. I imagine yours do, too.

I am the wind on the sea
I am the wave of the sea
I am the bull of seven battles
I am the eagle on the rock
I am a flash from the sun
I am the most beautiful of plants
I am a strong wild boar
I am a salmon in the water
I am a lake in the plain
I am the word of knowledge
I am the head of the spear in battle
I am the God that puts fire in the head
Who spreads light in the gathering on the hills?
Who can tell the ages of the moon?
Who can tell the place where the sun rests?
(Song of Amergin, transl. Lady Augusta)

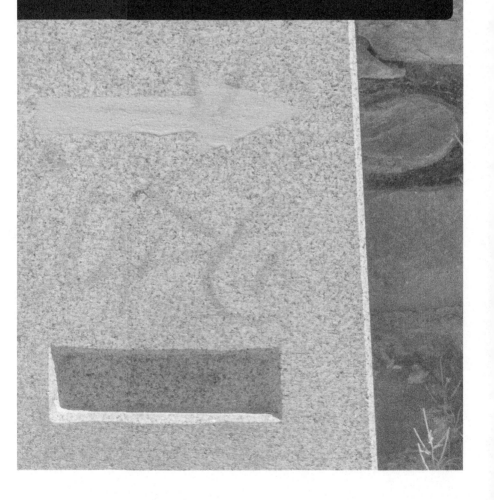

OUR PRACTICES

Daily prayer is the core of this practice. As written in the Rule: "Constantly pray," and "Be constant in your vigils, from eve to eve." Prayer is the communication by which we commune with the holy and by which the Divine communes with us. It is, in essence, the way in which we embody the sacred calling to monastic practice.

Daily prayer encompasses a wide variety of actions. Saying (or singing) the Office of the Hours is only one aspect of daily prayer, albeit a key one. Other aspects of daily prayer include silence; spontaneous prayer; meditation, including the use of prayer beads; and turning our work into prayer; such as the knitting of a prayer shawl or acting as the hands of our Patrons through volunteer work.

Silence is vital because it is only through silence that we can truly listen to the voice of the Divinities when They speak to us. Silence is difficult to achieve in our contemporary culture, where our secular culture often values a facsimile of business over depth of thought and practice. Silence is also a thorny issue when we are people who have so much work to do and only so many hours in the day.

However, even taking a few minutes of silence each day, to listen and to be with the world, can be radically transformative. Silence can be found in unexpected place. Sitting on the train into work, breathing alone in the car before going into the grocery store, at the table before a midafternoon snack, or in the shower before readying for your day, silence is available to all of us. We need only reach out and partake of it.

Spontaneous prayer is when we reach out to our Gods and Powers unexpectedly and in the moment. These can be prayers of thanksgiving or petitionary prayers or even quiet moments of praise and devotion. Through monastic practice and regular prayer, such spur-of-the-moment prayers will begin to come naturally to many people and we should always follow through on the sudden, impulsive desire to reach out to the Divine.

Reaching out to the Divinities and Powers is something the monastic practitioner should do. They have called us to give ourselves over to Them. It stands to reason that They are also listening to us. Thank Them for big and small things – getting a parking spot during the Christmas rush at the mall and for access to life-saving medical treatment in a crisis. Ask for Their protection and guidance likewise – in preparation for a big test in school and when going into an active warzone. And always praise Them when the thought comes to mind.

Mediation is related to silence, but it is a little more active. Depending upon the style of meditation(s) a monastic practitioner uses, it can either be a way to reach out to the spirits and Powers or a way to listen to them. Ideally, if one uses meditation as another way of reaching out and speaking to the Powers, another form of meditation should be used to listen to Them. It is very easy, in our hectic modern lives, to forget to listen to the voices from the Otherworld.

The use of prayer beads, while deeply associated in America with the Catholic (or Anglican) rosary and Buddhist malas, is a world-wide phenomena. It is a kind of meditation that relies on repetitive action, namely moving the prayer beads through one's hand as the devotee recites either a mantra or prayers associated with each bead. This form of repetitive prayer is surprisingly soothing and, with regular usage, one can easily memorize a prayer or sets of prayer, according to one's need and calling.

There are several online venues who sell Deity and tradition specific prayer beads. Generally, they are made by artists, rather than commercial distributors, so keep that in mind when seeking them out. It is also possible to make one's own prayer beads after a quick trip to the local craft or jewelry store. I personally have one set of prayer beads that were bought and one set I made myself. I find I use the one I made for daily meditation during my work commute.

We can also turn our work, whether it is paid work or volunteering or simply our hobbies, into vital acts of prayer. By offering up our daily tasks, chores and beloved hobbies alike, to the Powers who have called us, we can turn the everyday minutia into constant, ongoing prayers. This choice and skill is at heart of what it means to have joined into monastic practice. This is a very real way of giving over to the Divinities while living outside of a cloister.

There are several customs, in addition to daily prayer, that allow for a consistent routine that specifically honors this special call to monastic practice. Some forms of the daily prayer, such as the usage of prayer beads and the specifics of the Daily Office, which are worthy of further illumination. This next section will deal with these.

Our Shrines and Homes of the Holy

It is a worthy task, when one takes on the role of monastic practitioner, to create a place in one's home set aside for prayer and worship. When prayer is a daily practice, it is much easier to develop a healthy, prayerful habit when there is already a place to do so. Just as it can be difficult to set out to write a novel without a desk, so too is it difficult to become a monk without a place to honor one's Gods, Powers, and calling.

Often when we think about places to prayer, in the world of polytheism and neopaganism, we immediately imagine either a Wiccan-style or ceremonial magic altar or the casting of circles of protection before entering into a working. A home shrine can be an elaborate centerpiece of the room, decorated with a fine altar cloth, statuary, fine candles, and sacramental tools. However this is not necessarily the universal understanding of a shrine or holy place and, sometimes, such elaborate garlanding can actually take away from the true usage of the shrine.

I have kept shrines for many years and they all vary according to space and need. Any shared space, such as a family home, must be taken into account for those who are building and tending to their first shrines. If there is a shared household practice, even one as broad as a general polytheist household, it will be easier to have an open negotiation about space that may be allotted for shrines and prayer space. If one is not open about one's practices or belief systems are already a source of tension in the household, it may be easier to privately designate a small space in an area that already belongs to the practitioner, such as a shelf above a desk or a corner of side table.

It is good to think of a shrine or place of prayer as the home for the Divine within our homes, offices, and lives in general. By building a deliberate space for prayer and worship in our homes and lives, we are inviting the Holy to join with us in a special way. In this way, too, should the home shrine be specific. Rather than a single working altar devoted to magical practice, Deities and powers should have individual spaces. These spaces can be as small as a candle holder or bookend and as large as a small table, but, by separating them, we honor the multiplicity of Holy that we honor and venerate.

Shrines can and should start small. We are adamantly not in need of the elaborate and specific tools of the ceremonial magician. This is a practice of prayer and rule; thus a simple, private space for prayer, where we can reflect and honor the Powers and spirits, can often best mirror what we do. It is easier to get into the correct headspace when our environs imitate our practice.

For the person who has either limited space or limited ability to openly observe, a small shrine and space for prayer will be easy, inexpensive, and enlightening. A bookshelf of poetry with a bookend in the shape of a lamb or posy of snowdrops would be perfectly workable for someone seeking out devotion with Brigid and space can be made even in a college dorm or studio apartment. By the same token, someone connecting to the Holy Dead might clear out the top of a bureau and decorate with a dark rock, representing the House of Donne, and three fabric or paper apple blossoms, to represent the Otherworld. Such a place of worship can even be made into a travel shrine. The possibilities are endless with a little bit of creativity.

A larger shrine can be a little more elaborate and may be desirable for those who openly practice and have the space. My current shrine to Manannan mac Lir is a repurposed end table in the living room. With an altar cloth made of some spare fabric, two framed pictures made by friends, a found conch shell, silver bowl in the shape of a shell, and a brass candle holder, the end table by the couch became a place of prayer. As that is where I perform the daily Office of the Hours, it seemed appropriate to develop a shrine there.

Travel shrines can also be useful, whether for the person whose life takes them away from home often or for the person who would rather carry their place of prayer with them throughout the day. With a portable shrine, any place – a coffee shop, your work cubicle, a hotel room in a distant city – can suddenly become the place where you can deeply connect and communication with your Deities, spirits, and powers.

A place of prayer or shrine should be always well maintained and, for this reason if no other, one should make sure not to make them so elaborate as to require extensive daily maintenance. Offerings, such as food, liquids, or plant material, should be exchanged for new offerings as appropriate and the previous items disposed of. Liquids can, of course, be poured out as libations and plant material and other natural materials returned to nature. Food, however, should not be consumed as in many later fairy and folk traditions, food left out to the spirits lost its nutritive power and taking back an offering was viewed very poorly. Generally, I recommend that this be done weekly, if not on a daily basis.

A good time to reconsider shrines and places of prayer and to rearrange them, as well as maintaining issue such as ash from burnt offerings such as incense and pooled wax from burning candles, is a holy day. Because we are already considering the Holy and Divine and our relationship to

Them on a holy day or holiday, it is natural to work on these days to make sure that their shrines, or homes in our homes, are appropriately prepared for Their presences. At this time, one may add a seasonal decoration, suitable to the holiday; change the altar cloth; add or subtract decoration, such as candles, devotional figures, and written prayers.

The act of keeping a place of worship in our homes is an act of prayer unto itself. It is a very physical way to demonstrate our veneration of that Holy which lives in and emanates from the shrine. For this reason, and because routine and habit are a crucial part of monastic practice, daily prayers said at the shrine, as well as daily offerings and devotions offered at the shrine, create a world of prayer or holiness around these spaces. You may find yourself looking at your end table or shelf of poetry differently after building a shrine out of it.

Our Offerings

Offerings are an aspect of prayer that is often neglected in modern Westernized culture, much to our detriment. Offerings, while the word might conjure the image of the animal sacrifices of the pre-modern world, can be many things and will often vary according to the desires of the Holy One to whom we offer and our relationship to that Power. By entering into a monastic practice, in many ways, we are offering one of the great sacrifices we can: we offer ourselves.

Offerings and prayer are so similar in work and practice that it is hard to separate them and, indeed, the attempt may entirely be futile. Often sacramental prayer is an offering made, as with the Christian Eucharist. When we turn our work into a prayer, becoming the hands of the Divine in this world, we are making a huge offering. When we choose silence and to listen to Their voices, we are giving our voices and direction over to Them as an offering.

However, when polytheists and neopagans talk about offerings, they often mean a very specific subset of offerings that are commonly given over to our Gods and Powers and can, in many ways, create a wonderful visual cue to ourselves and those who see us perform our duties, signaling that these Great Powers are worthy of sacrifice. The most common forms of these might be incense, candles, and liquid libations.

In a monastic practice, we do not "give one to get one." We are answering a sacred calling, entering into an uneven contract with Something (or Someone) far greater than ourselves, Someone so unknowable and yet deeply intimate that we can only call them Divine. They have called us and we have answered, stepping into that oarless coracle and allowing Them to direct it. The offerings and sacrifices we make to Them are reflective of that relationship, often just on a much smaller scale, on that we can see on a day to day basis.

It is also a part of hospitable practice. Hospitality was important in the ancient Celtic world and it is important to us today. We trust in the Powers and spirits to be hospitable as we navigate through our world with Their aid. When we invite Them into our homes, through prayer and shrine building and religious rites, we have become, in many ways, their hosts. Just as we offer a glass of water to a friend visiting our home, so, too, is it only hospitable to offer a bowl of water at a shrine before prayer.

Liquid offerings are the most common ones that I offer at my household shrines. Almost every shrine, but not all, has a chalice or bowl and a place for it. Whether it is a silver bowl of salted water at Manannán's shrine before entering into the Morning Office or pouring hot tea in an earthenware chalice and offering it the Holy Dead before I prepare my own mug, these are simple, inexpensive offerings that nonetheless serve as a daily reminder of my relationship with Them. Milk and alcoholic offerings also occupy traditional spaces in the folklore coming to us from various Celtic lands. Particularly in Irish and Cornish fairy folklore, it was not uncommon to offer a little dish of milk and bread out after dark for the fairy folk.

Many offer forms of food to accompany their liquid offerings libations, thus creating something like a small meal for the Powers. Whether this is a full meal – protein, vegetables, and starches – or a piece of bread, as with that ubiquitous offering of dry bread in a dish of sweet milk, it can be a very satisfying offering. When offering food, the portions offered to the Powers and spirits now belongs to Them and is no longer appropriate to consume ourselves.

If we want to share a meal or snack with Them, we should simply be careful to designate what belongs to us and what belongs to Them. This has roots in folklore about food belonging or given to fairy folk, however it is also proper hospitality. Just as we should not eat from a guest's plate when we host a dinner party, so should we not be taking from the sacrifices we make to the Holy. We have an ethical obligation to be hospitable with the Divine as much as we do with our people in this world.

Burnt offerings, such as candles or incense, are another

common and accessible form of offering that can help set the tone for prayer and sacrament. While the details of it are beyond the purpose of this text, the making of one's own incense, appropriate to the offering, whether to a holy day or specific Deity, can make the offering that much deeper than burning store bought incense. Commercial incense, which is more easily accessible and can be more economical, is also an appropriate burnt offering. The lighting of fires has been associated with communion with the Holy since ancient times and, in our era of technology, we can also use electric and battery powered candles to do the same. Electricity is, after all, a harnessed form of fire.

Burnt offerings can also take the form of burnt plant materials, if the practitioner has access to an appropriate fire-safe space, such as a clean, functioning fireplace or a functioning fire pit in a yard. Pleasant smelling or spiritually associated wood, such as apple wood or mesquite, can be burned in a fireplace. In a fire pit or similar place, where concerns about resins such as creosote and their residues can be put to the side, one can burn a wider variety of offerings, such as pine cones, or throw mineral salts onto the fire, which can temporarily change the color of the flame.

When making offerings of this type, it is important to remain within our budgets and be realistic in how often we can make them. A bowl of water or dram of tea, a piece of a homemade loaf of bread or timed lighting of an electric candle, are probably more realistic, particularly for the practitioner without much disposable income. These are offerings that simply are a part of our days already. We merely invite the Divine to join us in that cup of tea or fresh loaf of bread.

I generally reserve more lavish offerings, such as libations of mead or whiskey or other alcoholic beverage, for holy days. These are days that have already been taken out of the calendar and elevated with a purpose. On these days, perhaps, a greater sacrifice may be called for. At these times, too, I generally offer them in the context of a larger liturgy with a group of people, so that we are all making the offering together. It is not merely my own hands that make oblation to the Powers, but the hands and souls of the whole group.

Holidays and the Wheel of the Year

The Wheel of the Year, as it commonly used and understood in the neopagan community, is a 20th century esoteric invention of Ross Nichols and Gerald Gardner, with only loose ties to its supposed historical grounding in very real Celtic and Anglo-Saxon holidays. However, being a modern invention is not, inherently, a bad thing and a reason to reject it out of hand. Much of modern religious custom, if it is to serve the spiritual and social needs of contemporary society, must be created in our modern world, rather than drawn directly from the worlds of pre-Christian Europe.

Especially if we are looking at the historical Celtic world for our development holidays, we are once again confronted by the limitations of the written record. All of our written record for the cultural practices of the ancient Celtic world is directly filtered through the lens of the Celtic and Roman Catholic Christian monastic system. This means two things. One, our understanding of the holidays is immediately viewed through the early Christian calendar, which is rife with small and large holidays, from minor saints' day to major tides, such as Michaelmas and Whitsuntide. The second is that, although the monks and nuns of Ireland,

Wales, and Scotland were certainly Celtic in culture and attitude, the Celts of the Second Golden Age were far from the First Golden Age and thus, they add an extra layer of distance and interpretation.

Of course, we do have archaeological evidence, for those who have their hearts set on at least understanding the holidays by which our Gods and Powers were honored in previous millennia. The Neolithic tomb complex at Bru Na Boinne, of course, shows a complex mathematical understanding of the movement of the sun and different sections align with the autumnal equinox, the winter solstice, and the spring equinox. However, even though this is proof that these times of year had significance of some kind for Neolithic people residing in the Boyne valley, probably a pre-Celtic people, it does not tell us what that significance was nor how they celebrated it, if they celebrated at all.

This does not mean that we do not have holidays. It means that we can look at the folklore and medieval storytelling tradition and the modern esoteric neo-pagan holiday calendar. They can meld together well. After all, Ross Nichols and Gerald Gardner, however a modern monastic practitioner may feel about them (good or bad), were not developing their practices in a vacuum.

Holidays, or holy days, comprise an important aspect of the monastic tradition, particularly one deriving, at least in part, from the ongoing Celtic monastic tradition. Holy days are way markers throughout the year, signaling changes in prayer and liturgy. For the polytheist, holy tides and the seasonal tides they mark can signal a change in Who we honor, individually and as groups. Certainly, in my own practice, while I have particular closeness to certain Powers, the high holy days belong specifically to the worship and honor of Powers associated with those days.

In addition to the standard holidays that would be shared by most everyone – and shared by many non-monastic practicing neopagans and polytheists – it is also good for the monastic practitioner to add holidays that may be of particular importance to their Gods and Powers. For example, while midsummer is often a solar holiday celebrated by neopagans, I specifically recognize a day that falls, generally, between St John's Eve and July 4, where I follow the traditional Manx tribute to Manannan mac Lir and ritually "pay the rent" in the form of brightly colored flowers and eco-friendly little boats offered to the water.

There is a strong mythic and folk tradition, in both the medieval monastic texts that have survived and been translated and in the folklore and cultural traditions of the modern Celtic lands, to support the holidays of the so-called Fire Festivals: Samhain, Imbolc, Beltane, and Lughnasagh. Whether it is the burning of Tara at Samhain in the Finnian cycle or the folk practices of bonfires at Beltane according to folklorists such as Sir James Frazer, we can derive our own practices. From these we can develop an understanding of a modern polytheistic monastic view of these holy days.

It is generally accepted that Samhain, from October 31 to November 2, functions as the end and beginning of the year, just as December 31 to January 1 does in our secular calendar. It has specific folk associations with the Otherworld and the dead. Potentially part of the reason the Roman Catholic Church celebrates All Saint's and All Soul's Day at this time, Samhain was often a time for people to pay respect for the dead and practice ritual (including folk ritual such as guising) to ward off any malicious intent coming from the Otherworld.

Modern practices include singing the Office of the Dead, as part of the special prayers set aside for the evening and morning of Samhain. In addition to the special Offices written for each holiday, we have devotional practices that may be associated with the Gods and Otherworldly powers for each day. On Samhain, we might pay tribute to Donne, for the dead, and psychopomps, such as the Morrigan, as well as our own honored dead. This can take the form of specific prayers, but also ritual offerings, dumb suppers, celebrations of food with family and friends, and, of course, partaking in masking and wearing of costumes. This can be a very festive holiday, celebrating the turning of the year and the souls that are close, as the veil to the Otherworld thins.

Holidays other than Samhain are often treated as purely agricultural in nature, however they can be viewed through a mystic, devotional, or monastic lens instead. While Celtic culture was agricultural for a very long time – the industrial revolution was often denied to colonial holdings and, when it did arrive, they did not control it – most, if not all, monastic practitioners do not and will not live an agricultural or agrarian lifestyle. Many of us, especially those reading an e-reader version of this text, live in countries and regions that have experienced the technological revolution. While we should follow the seasons and tides of the seasons, our experience of them and our experience of direct dependence on personal harvest (or lack thereof) necessitate that we do not celebrate holy days in the same way as an agrarian society or subsistence farmers.

Imbolc, associated with St Brigid's Day and the lambing and

calving season in Ireland, is the high holy day that follows Samhain. Celebrated at the turn of January to February in the Gregorian calendar of the Northern Hemisphere, the seasonality of the day will vary according to the bioregion of the monastic practitioner. However, when many of us will not be celebrating the lambs and calves that bring increase and wealth to our herds, we can still celebrate other aspects of Brigid, to whom this holy day belongs.

I often take this day to bless and sain water for the coming year, especially if it is well water or snow water. Depending on one's region, a practitioner may be able to celebrate the first flowers of spring, especially the snowdrop or crocus, or the warmth of the fire that still protects us from winter's dangerous cold, even if it is an electric fire. Young mothers may honor Brigid as their special protector and patron of their babies. Honoring the aspects of Brigid that affect our lives, both at this specific holy time and in an ongoing manner, is a wonderful way to express holiday devotions.

Beltane, or May Day, traditionally marked the times that, after a bonfire blessing, the herds were driven up to high pasture for the summer. After Beltane, the youths who looked after the cattle and sheep herds would leave their families and villages behind and live at the high pasture, a practice in Ireland known as booleying. In some regions, you can still see the booley houses where they slept. It was also a time that often marked when the Fianna and others would move from their own winter grounds to their summer outlawry. This, too, was often celebrated as a mirror to Samhain as the Otherworld was close, although this was a time when Spirits and Powers were more likely to cross over, rather than the souls of the dead.

While we will not be, for the most part, moving our herds for summer, we can sain ourselves between two fires, be they a pair of traditional bonfires or two candles on a pair of end tables. By passing through the fire and smoke, we prepare ourselves (and possibly any pets who are amenable to a saining) for the coming seasons. In theory, too, this is another ritualized protection from any malicious intent of Otherworldly spirits. We can also collect appropriate seasonal food and ritual tools, such as early berries and young greenery, even if we purchase them at a farmer's market. It is a good time to retell stories from the Fenian and Ossian cycles.

Lughnasadh is a festal holiday often celebrated at the same time as Lammas or Loaf Mass, at the end of July or beginning of August. The folklore for this holiday is somewhat varied. Many neopagan sources reference Lugh holding a funeral games for his foster mother Tailtiu at this time, although, of course, the fosterage of Lugh is a tale that varies by region and storyteller for the past thousand years. In modern time,s Lughnasadh has been a holiday in Ireland celebrated by specific pilgrimages, regional festival and fairs, and family reunions.

It is, of course, a time to celebrate the harvest, but, as Lughnasadh often falls in the Dog Days of summer for many of us in American bioregions, we are not yet prepared for autumn and the associated harvests of hay and grain that may already be occurring in other regions. It can, then, be a day or days to enjoy the fruits of the summer harvest, such as maize, sweet berries, garden treasures, or fresh herbs. In addition to the special holiday Office of the Hours, it may also be a time to participate in races, dances, and other interactive competitions in honor of Lugh, the warrior who led the Tuatha de Danaan to victory over the Fomorians, His mother's people. It is also a good time for traditional reunions of loved ones and celebrations of the season.

These I treat as High Holidays, holy days that require not merely a special set of prayers and office, but special attitudes, practices, and gatherings with like minded polytheistic or neo-pagan friends. As Fire Festivals, they take a primacy only because they have strong folk context, even through the latter era. The other celebrations on the Wheel of the Year, the solar festivals, have some archeological evidence and can be tied, with little effort, to Christian holidays, such as Christmastide and Michaelmas, despite having at least some historical in Anglo-Saxon and Germanic practices.

These holidays, beginning at the Winter Solstice and moving through the growth, peak, and ebb of the sun, supply smaller days. On these holy days, a more solitary monastic practitioner may simply take it as a special day of private dedication and the household or group practitioner can have a smaller holiday as one for smaller devotional gatherings, special offices of shared prayer, and particular offerings to the Gods and Powers of these days. Some of these days may belong to a Power or spirit of particular interest to a monastic practitioner and thus, can be held as a more important day for that person or household.

The winter solstice is a time to recognize the longest night of the year and enjoy the light of the other stars that decorate the heavens of this world and the Otherworld. As winter deepens, particularly in extreme northern and southern bioregions, this is a time to give homage to the Cailleach, or great winter hag who brings damaging and dangerous storms. At the same time, she may be a Spirit of devotion, for Her power and wisdom. It is also a time to fill the longest night with light, whether fire, candle, or electric, accompanied by a special Office of prayer.

The spring equinox, falling as it does halfway between Imbolc and Beltane, is a time to celebrate the balance of light and dark and, depending on one's bioregion, the life that is slowly returning to the field and meadow in the form of spring blooms. It is also a wonderful time to give devotion to Powers who aid in that growth, such as Airmed, daughter of Dian Cecht, who sought to teach the world of the healing powers of herbs and green life. There is great wisdom in the life that slowly creeps back into the meadows at early spring and we, as monastic practitioners, would do well to heed it as we honor spirits and Powers in our devotions.

The summer solstice is a time to rejoice in the height of the power of the sun and the coming summer that stretches before us at midsummer. The heat of the sun is at once a blessing, bringing life to the fields and the harvest, and a danger, one that might scorch us and the world around us. Traditionally, the people of Man would "pay the rent" at this time and it is a good moment to look to the spirits of the sea and waters and pay tribute. As with all holy days, special prayers and devotional may accompany monastic practice, marking it as a special day among days.

The autumnal equinox is again a time when the darkness and light are in precarious balance and a time to observe the fall, when the wild animals bring in their harvest from the field and organize for the long winter, even before our spiritual preparation at Samhain. This is the time to honor the opening of Angus Og's home at Bru Na Boinne, which will be unlocked now and at the winter solstice and the spring equinox. Particular Offices of prayer and offerings, appropriate to the holy day and Spirits to whom the holy day belongs, may be given, either individually or as a group.

Thus the Wheel of the Year, while rooted firmly in esoteric magical practice, can be successfully applied to a polytheistic Celtic monastic practice. This is not a reconstruction of any pre-conversion holy day calendar nor is it meant to be one. The monastic practice discussed in this texts, while having roots grounded in history, is not a reconstruction, but is designed to be a movement forward: a monastic practice that serves the needs of 21st century polytheists, if you will. ally to the worship and honor of Powers associated with those days. Divination

Our Divination within Daily Prayer
A.R. Blackthorn

The act of divination is more an art than a science. Symbols, be they bones, cards, or fews, are thrown and interpreted using some kind of system. Ultimately, any form of divination is about connecting the diviner (and querent if they are different) and the higher power of their intuitive mind. The more complex and robust systems like the Tarot are far more than fortune telling devices. They are keys to our personal and communal journey, a window to the Gods, and a road map to liberation and understanding of our own minds and souls.

In this style of monastic practice, we often perform some kind of simple oracular divination during the morning and sometimes the evening prayers. This is for two reasons. First, it helps us listen to our Gods, Powers and spirits, allowing them to speak to us more directly than they might in a moment of silent meditation. Second, it gives us insight into our day - symbols to look for and lessons to learn. This second reason is why an individual practitioner may choose to use apantomancy, or the chance happenings of the day or certain times of day, to understand their morning (or evening) communication with the Powers.

Any divinatory method one is comfortable with can be used, however this exercise is not about fortune telling. Some may be familiar with the idea of a Tarot reading or casting Ogham fews for themselves or a friend, but this oracular divination is fundamentally different at the root. This is a more direct use of the divination tool through oracular reading for connection with the spirits and the Powers with whom we commune in prayer.

The messages that come through can be clarion clear or muddy, but they are an attempt to listen to the voice of our best selves and the Shining Ones we worship. The point is not to gain direct, constant clean messages, but to engage in a style of communication and prayer where we listen at least as often as we speak. Divination is a time when we ask those Powers to speak to us and we can, if we so choose, take the time to be quiet and listen for Their messages and lessons for us.

There are some styles of divination that are more suited to this style of listening, rather than personal readings. Different kinds of divination will better suit different practitioners and these will rely both on one's personal experience with oracular divination and how one listens to the voices that come to us from the Otherworld. Choosing one style of divination over another is a matter of personal preference and not one that is related to one's suitability to monastic practice.

The Tarot

The Tarot decks that we use today are all direct descendants of the Western Mystery Tradition, the Golden Dawn, and in particular Arthur Edward Waite and Pamela "Pixie" Colman-Smith's deck, the Rider-Waite Tarot. Waite's goal was to create a deck that held all of the secrets of their tradition and could and should be used as a spiritual tool, and way of making contact with what he would have called our "Holy Guardian Angel". It is in this way that we can use the Tarot for an oracle and not merely divination (will he return my love? will I get the job?). For those familiar with using this style of divination cards, especially those with extensive training, it can be a very elegant, nuanced, beautiful system of soul language. For others, especially those who do not have access or time for the training required to understand the Tarot or the Rider-Waite system of symbolism, the Tarot may contain a level of complexity (or ties to Western esoteric magic) that are unwelcome in a system of daily prayer.

Oracle Cards
Oracle cards have a very different function than Tarot cards, although they are often sold alongside them and discussed in the same spaces. Rather they are a complete, closed system of oracular divination and each deck is read differently. They can provide excellent guides for direct Otherworldly communication because they are designed to make that connection to both oneself and the Great Powers. As each deck comes with its own understanding of communication and style, a practitioner should work independently to develop communication and communion with their deck.

The art styles are incredibly variable and one can generally find a deck or set of decks that speaks to one's own aesthetic. They also come in nearly any theme imaginable: Arthurian, Celtic, Norse, Egyptian, Fairy, Angels, Goddesses, Animals, Plants, and even Halloween themed decks. Each practitioner should choose a deck that speaks to one's own relationships, should they choose to use an oracle deck.

Fews and Stones
Both of the Celtic Ogham and Norse/Germanic runes rely on ancient holy alphabets carved into wood or stone to provide the means to divine. Although they can and are used for divination both the Ogham and the Runes are best used in applications like this as they both have historic and modern connections to the Gods of their traditions. Either

one stone or few is chosen from a bag or they are thrown as a group and interpreted that way with positions as an important factor. Due to the limited time frame for morning prayer, I recommend a single draw. For holidays and special days where time is no object, a more detailed card spread or throwing is appropriate.

For those practitioners who choose to use fews or stones as their method of oracular divination and communion with the Holy, they should also seek out a direct, deep understanding of these alphabets. Neither is easily understood at the outset of a practice and, outside of the ritual of daily prayer, one should set aside time to study and work with the stones or fews. They are ancient and complicated systems, which can be very rewarding and provide deeply insightful conversation, but they require a level of work akin to an academic understanding of the Tarot.

Bones or Shells
There are those who have developed their own oracular systems or developed a system based on a familial or indigenous system, often using bones, shells, or sticks. These are often deeply personal and arise with a practitioner's individual relationship with the animal or tree to whom that particular device belongs. Some specific traditions practice the throwing of bone dice or cowry shells that are then interpreted by the diviner.

These are perfectly appropriate for the monastic practitioner to use during the morning or evening office of prayer, given that they have enough time set aside to do a full reading. Depending on one's personal system, a reading of thrown bones, wood, or shells might take as much time as a traditional Tarot reading and, thus, be an impediment to a morning prayer before heading off to a lengthy morning commute. In these cases, a practitioner might consider using a personal system when they have the time, such as in the evening or on a weekend, and choose a more expedient practice, such as an online oracle deck, for a morning office. These decisions will always be personal, but the ideal is to make sure that the office of prayer is accessible and attainable at all times.

Using the Oracles for Morning Prayer

The most important aspect of the "morning/evening card" or "morning/evening rune" (or "morning/evening reading") for an oracular purpose is the interpretation the oracle and the overall intention. The questions that are often asked in a divinatory reading are generally personal and relatively specific, such as "How will my love life evolve over the next month?". Oracular questions in the office of prayer are very different and require a shift in both language and intention

Here are some guidelines:
Avoid yes/no questions.
Ask general prayerful questions directed specifically to the Holy and Divine.
Give the oracle a wide range so it can address what the Gods want you to know rather than a preconceived notion of an answer.
Examples
Don't ask "Will I be in a relationship with x person?"
Do ask "What do I need to know for today?"
Don't ask "Will x happen to me today?"
Do ask "What guides and guidelines should I seek out today?"
Don't ask "Should I make this choice?"

Do ask "What are the best things for me to do today?"

Remember always that the goal is to communicate with the spirits, Powers and Deities. Sometimes the question is less of an articulated sentence and more of a long moment of quiet listening, followed by the drawing of a card, few, or stone. The more we practice the more Their messages can become clear.

Finally, and most importantly, know that the future is cast in sand. This practice of oracular divination is not a matter of reading the future or seeing what will happen. There is no notion that the Celts historically believed in anything that mirrors the Greek Fate or the Norse Wyrd and this practice is not meant to foresee either of those.

This process is only meant to facilitate a strong communication with Those who have called us to this practice. Too often, even when we have developed a habit of regular prayer, we engage in a pattern of only speaking, but never listening; only asking, and never offering; only doing, and never waiting. The practice of daily, and often twice daily, practicing oracular divination is a moment when we can step away from that and listen, hear, and process what the Gods and Powers are saying to us.

Prayer Beads

There are many wonderful texts on the making of prayer beads. They are superb and those who have written them have far more experience making jewelry than I do. If a monastic practitioner desires to make a set of prayer beads (or multiple sets), I highly recommend picking up one of several books on pagan prayer beads for instruction and inspiration. Having beads that you have designed and chosen can make a difference in one's willingness to use them in daily prayer.

Prayer beads should generally be dedicated to either one God or Power or a set of Gods or Powers. (For examples, it is perfectly appropriate to consecrate a set of beads to the Morrigan and to Badb, Macha, and Nemain.) Once given over to these spirits or Powers, it is wise for the practitioner to reserve their usage to be in honor, homage, and communion with those self same Powers and Spirits.

While each monastic practitioner, by designing their own beads according to both their own comfort and the devotion of their Calling, will be unique among their peers, there are some general recommendations in both the beads themselves and the prayers associated with them. While these are suggestions and guidelines, not rules handed down by an authority, I have tried many styles of prayer and prayer bead over the years and these come from years of experience.

Repetitive, rote prayer is often ideal for use with prayer beads. These can be as simple as single word mantras associated with the God or Power to whom the beads belong or multilineal prayers, memorized over time by the monastic practitioner. Some fixed prayers have already been written and can be found in devotional books or at extant shrines. Some may be adapted from historical poetic sources. Others will need to be written by monastic practitioners who experience direct mystical inspiration from the Powers who have called them.

While rote prayer often occupies a lesser place in neo-pagan and polytheistic circles, it offers very specific benefits when applied to prayer beads. Repeating the same lines or mantras while handling the prayer beads allows the monastic practitioner to enter a liminal state, where they no longer think about each word in the prayer, as the reader does when reading a line, but is allowed to absorb the full meaning of the prayer or mantra and enter into a sacred space where they can encounter the holy. By repeating themselves and becoming lost in the greater meaning, the monastic practitioner can find new ways to communicate with the Divine. Combining breathing practices, such as the four fold breath, with fixed, rote prayer can aid with this kind of state, if it is desired.

Because of this semi-altered state that can be induced by the combination of fixed prayer and the use of prayer beads, if the monastic practitioner desires multiple mantras or multiple fixed prayers on one set of beads, it is advisable to use beads of different sizes or textures to indicate a change in prayer or mantra. In this way, the prayer beads are a tactile experience offered up in ecstasy to the Holy, as well as a form of meditation.

The Daily Office

In the next section there is the Daily Office, in the form
of three liturgies. There is an extended morning office, a
limited midday office, and an extended evening office. This
is designed to map onto a typical day, where extended offices
can be performed at home before and after the rush of the
day, while the limited midday office is a call for quiet prayer
that can fit into a lunch break.

Each Office begins and ends with matching prayers:
In the name of the land that supports us,
In the name of the sky vaulted above us,
And in the name of the great sea that surrounds us.

I actually use this prayer as a form of verbal saining,
or entering into the sacred space that allows for true
communication with the Holy. Even for more expansive
liturgies, such as holiday celebrations for Imbolc or
Lughnasadh, I always open and close with the same prayers.
This has allowed this specific prayer to indicate to me and
those in this practice that we are automatically entering (or
leaving) sacred space with this prayer. It's effective enough
that I will sometimes use it to get in the right headspace for
another type of prayer or work, such as meditation.

This is followed by the full office prayer, which varies
appropriately according to the time of days. The Morning
Prayer is both a saining to prepare for the day, a thanksgiving
for the morning, and a dedication of the day. If one desires
and has time, it can be appropriate to sain with incense or
dried herbs during the part. The Midday Prayer is quick
office of thanksgiving, for both the day and the midday
meal. The Evening Prayer is a second saining followed by
a dedication of the body and soul in repose. As with the

Morning Prayer, if the practitioner has the time, space, and inclination, it can be fitting to sain oneself with lit incense, a bundle of burning herbs, or even a hanging censer.

After the opening, the Morning and Evening Prayer ask for a reading. For those familiar with the traditional Daily Offices, this is directly drawn from them. However, we have no Bible from which to source psalms or Gospel readings. This is perfectly alright. I typically allow this reading to be a topical poem or piece of folklore. There are several compendiums of poetry and folklore online as well as free and low cost apps for electronic devices, so finding readings does not need to be a financial investment. Please be sure to include folklore and poetry that would be of specific interest to your tradition, Deities, and life. Many of my poets are queer and much of my folklore is Irish, but this may not best reflect your life.

This is then followed by a moment of meditation. The Midday Prayer only has a moment of meditation between the opening and closing prayers because it seems unwieldy, to me, to carry poetry and folklore with me for what is a work break. For those who do not work or who have the time to add to their Midday prayer, they are welcome to do so.

The meditation is just a moment of silence, rather than a time for mantras or chanting. I may reflect on the preceding reading, but more often, I attempt to take it as fleeting moment of true quiet, silence in sacred space. So often when we are in the liminality of sacred space, we are doing – praying, singing, telling stories, doing magic. This is time, three times a day, to simply be silent with the Holy.

After this, I write that we draw divination. As was discussed in a previous section, this is a different practice than doing a fortune telling reading unto itself. The choice of divination type is up to the monastic practitioner, but should be appropriate to the setting.

O spirits, give me of Thy abundance,
Ai, give me of Thy wisdom,
Niamh, give me in my need,
Banba beneath the shelter of Thy shield.
I lie down to-night,
With thy shared strength,
With Ai, with Niamh and with Banba,
With the Spirits of might tonight.
(traditional prayer, adapted)

OUR REGULAR OFFICES

The aim of the daily office is not simply to say rote and formulaic prayers, in the style of a mindless drone, but to have a regular, habitual manner by which one can communicate with the Divine. These regular offices - three daily offices in addition to the offices of the dead and an office of healing - are offered here not as a definitive manner of monastic prayer and asceticism, but as an option. The movement toward a polytheistic monastic practice, at the time of this writing, still appears to be new in the modern world, so I give this text as an offering both to the Holy and to the people seeking the Holy.

This is how I practice, in my own household practice of devotion. The individual called to an eremitic practice or a mendicant practice may find that these prayers and offices do not suit them. This is possible and I encourage those practitioners to develop the habits and prayers that suit their own Holy calling. These are what, right now, serve mine.

These prayer, generally speaking, are derived from Celtic Christian sources, including the Carmina Gadelica and prayers traditionally attributed to Celtic monastic saints or monasteries, much as other prayers in this text have been adapted. Some prayers written here been created independently and utterly by inspiration, but these are offices carrying forth a tradition thousands of years old. Conversion and belief change in waves, but practices and systems can withstand those changes.

I have written all of the prayers in the plural (we/us). I typically pray the morning and evening offices as part of a household prayer and the midday prayer, while said silently and alone, I understand to encompass more than just myself. For the solitary practitioner, it may be appropriate to adapt these into the singular (I/me) although it is worth considering and discerning if one is truly alone in prayer and what that means before doing so. As stated previously in this text, we function in a cosmology where we are very rarely truly alone. If these offices work for you, please use them. If they do not, please adapt them. But, by all means, do not understand them to be a be-all-and-end-all of a monastic prayer system or polytheistic Celtic office of prayer. They are but a step on the journey.

Our Office of Morning Prayer

In the name of the land that supports us,
In the name of the sky vaulted above us,
And in the name of the great sea that surrounds us,
We enter into prayer.

The sain, this morning, of the nine waves
Sain from death, sain from wound
Sain from breast to knee
Sain from knee to foot
Sain of the three sains
Sain of the nine sains
Sain of the twenty-seven sains
From the crown of the head
To the soles of the feet
Be the helmet of knowledge about our heads
Be the beads of peace about our throats
Be breastplate of the priest upon our breasts
To shield us this day and all days.

Reading
Moment of Silence
Oracular Divination

Thanks unto the powers and gods
Who brought us from yesterday
To the beginning of today.
Everlasting joy
To earn for our soul
With good intent
And forever gift of peace
Bestowed upon us.
Our thoughts, our words,

Our deeds and our desires
We dedicate to peace
We dedicate to silence
We dedicate to hospitality
We dedicate to powers, visible and invisible
Keep us from offence
And shield us through this day
For the sake of our communion
For the sake of our shared devotion.

In the name of the land that supports us,
In the name of the sky vaulted above us,
And in the name of the great sea that surrounds us,
We enter into the world.

Our Office of Midday Prayer

In the name of the land that supports us,
In the name of the sky vaulted above us,
And in the name of the great sea that surrounds us,
We enter into prayer.

Let the beauty of the sun be upon us,
Blessing the work of our bodies
Blessing the work of our hands
Blessing the work of our minds.

Moment of Silence

I give thanks for this sacrificial meal
To the spirits of the waters that quench my thirst
To the spirits of the green world that sate my hunger
To the spirits of the animals kind that sate my hunger
To the land herself who supports us all
I give thanks, I give great thanks

In the name of the land that supports us,
In the name of the sky vaulted above us,
And in the name of the great sea that surrounds us,
We enter into the world.

Our Office of Evening Prayer

In the name of the land that supports us,
In the name of the sky vaulted above us,
And in the name of the great sea that surrounds us,
We enter into prayer.

Sain and shield and sanctify us this night
O Elements and Powers, be seated at our helm
And lead us into peace at the end of our journey
With winds mild, kindly, benign, pleasant
Without swirl, without whirl, without eddy
That would do no harmful deed to us
We ask all these things of You
According to Your own will and words.

Moment of Silence
Oracular Divination (optional)

In our deeds
In our words
In our wishes
In our reason
And in the fulfilling of our desires
In our sleep
In our dreams
In our repose
In our thoughts
In our hearts and souls always
May the blessed and holy powers
And the promised Branch of Glory dwell
      O in our hearts and souls always
      May the blessed and holy powers
      And the fragrant Branch of Glory dwell.

In the name of the land that supports us
In the name of the sky vaulted above us
And in the name of the great sea that surrounds us
We enter into the world.

Our Offices of Healing

These are general offices to be used by all practitioners as necessary. When praying for oneself or someone in particular, please include their name and particular need in the statements before each prayer. These can be as simple as "Today we ask for [name] who is experiencing [illness]" or as complicated as adding a special poem invoking a deity in the name of the petitioner, depending on the comfort, need, and time available to the person saying the office.

The Office of Healing should be held as often as a practitioner desires, although ideal days include the day of the new moon and the spring equinox. For those who may have particular connections to healing deities or be in particular need of healing, it is not inappropriate to designate a particular day of the week, especially Wednesday or Saturday, to be a day for the office of healing. It can be added to any daily office or held at a different part of the day. If the office is being held for a particular person who is in need of healing, their name also can be invoked at the beginning of each separate prayer.

There are two sets of related Offices of Healing here. They should be used according to personal need, but each practitioner should attend to healing as they are personally called. The Office of Healing is more personal than the daily offices. It can and should be used for healing the practitioner themselves, for invoking healing for others in a practitioner's life, and for the healing of the world.

Our First Office of Healing

In the name of the land that supports us
In the name of the sky vaulted above us
And in the name of the great sea that surrounds us
We enter into prayer.

We believe in Gods and Powers who heal us and guide us
into the Otherworld, just as they guide us and teach us in
this world. Thus we prayer and ask for their aide in our times
of need. Today, we ask for the presence of Airmed and her
brother Miach, for little Manannan mac Lir, and for Brigid
of well and fire.

Light a candle as you speak

As Airmed and Miach sang over Nuada's ruined arm, we
sing today:
Bone to bone
Vein to vein
Balm to balm
Sap to sap
Skin to skin
Tissue to tissue
Blood to blood
Flesh to flesh
Sinew to sinew
Marrow to marrow
Pith to pith
Fat to fat
Membrane to membrane
Fiber to fiber
Moisture to moisture.

Light a candle as you speak

Little Manannan, son of Lir, who has restored great heros
and pilgrims, sustaining them beyond their earthly life, we
call to You with this rune:
This rune made by your people and your tribe in need
To the great little mariner,
For the wound, for illness, for malady here
For the nine painful diseases, for the three venomous diseases,
Refuse it not to us, deny it not to any.
As You went on a horse, Enbarr of the flowing mane,
He broke his leg on the shore,
So You went down,
You made the leg whole.
As You made whole that,
May You make whole this,
And more than this,
If it be Your will so to do.

Light a candle as you speak

Brigid, too, is a great and wondrous healer, with the
knowledge of the flame and the well. So we sing:
Blessed Brid went out
In the morning early,
With a pair of lambs;
One broke his leg,
With much ado,
That was apart,
She put bone to bone,
She put flesh to flesh,
She put sinew to sinew,
She put vein to vein;
As She healed that
May She heal this.

May these Great Powers be present and give guidance and healing, whatever that may be.
May pain be eased and souls soothed by their presence here with us.
May we know joy and communion even with illness and pain.

May we always know that we are not alone.
May They give us comfort in our darkest hours.
May They always shine a light that we may move forward.

May we know that healing sometimes comes in unexpected ways.
May we heal spiritually when we cannot heal physically.
My we always ask for help, even when we doubt it is available.

In the name of the land that supports us
In the name of sky vaulted above us
In the name of the great sea that surrounds us
We enter into the world.

Our Second Office of Healing

In the name of the land that supports us
In the name of the sky vaulted above us
And in the name of the great sea that surrounds us,
We enter into prayer.

Airmed, who mourns Your brother, who seeks to teach us
what we do not know of the green life that surrounds us, we
call on You. As You and Miach healed Nuada's severed hand,
heal us who stand here in Your name. Join us, teach us, guide
us.

Airmed went out
In the morning early,
With a pair of calves to break;
One broke his leg,
With much ado,
That was apart,
She put bone to bone,
She put flesh to flesh,
She put sinew to sinew,
She put vein to vein;
As she healed that
May she heal this.

Manannan, Lord of the Ninth Wave and bearer of the
sacred apple branch, You can bring peace and surety to any
You approach. Your music brings joy, love, and sorrow to the
world. As You have soothed those who have gone before us,
we ask that You bring that succor with You now.

We will pluck the yarrow fair,

That more peace shall be in us,
That more calm shall be in us,
That more honor shall be in us,
Be our speech the beams of the sun,
Be our lips the sap of the apple tree
May we be an isle in the sea,
May we be a hill on the shore,
May we be a star in waning of the moon,
May we be a staff to the weak,
Wounded can be every man,
Wound can no man we.

Bless Brigid three, healer, smith, and poet, You are the
bringer of healing and new life. It is by Your day that we
know spring is coming and it is by Your presence we know
that healing, by fire, has begun. We ask for Your presence,
Your aid, and Your Divine intervention today.

The charm put by Bride the beneficent,
On her goats, on her sheep, on her people,
On her horses, on her chargers, on her herds,
Early and late going home, and from home.
To keep us from rocks and ridges,
From the heels and the horns of one another
From the birds of the Red Rock,
And from Luath of the Feinne.
From the blue peregrine hawk of Creag Duilion,
From the brindled eagle of Ben-Ard,
From the swift hawk of Tordun,
From the surly raven of Bard's Creag.
From the fox of the wiles,
From the wolf of the Mam,
From the foul-smelling fumart,
And from the restless great-hipped bear.

From every hoofed of four feet,
And from every hatched of two wings
From every spirit of two feet.

In the name of the land that supports us,
In the name of the sky vaulted above us,
And in the name of the great sea that surrounds us,
We enter into the world

Offices of the Dead

We may say the office of the dead every month at the
new moon, making appropriate offerings according to
the season, astrological signs, and other omens according
to the practitioner. Candles may be lit and fitting incense
can include juniper, cedar, myrrh, cypress, nag champa,
rosemary, and bay. For the newly dead or honoring a specific
ancestor(s), their names should be invoked at the beginning
and end of the office.

Depending on a practitioner's relationship with the Mighty
Dead and death or Donne himself, one may offer the
Office of Dying more regularly. Saturday and Wednesday
may be appropriate days for a practitioner who is unsure.
Two litanies are offered and each should consider which is
appropriate for the situation. One may be sure for a funeral
or memorial service and another for a private litany for the
dead. This is up to the discretion of the practitioner

First Office of the Dead

In the name of the land that supports us
In the name of the sky vaulted above us
In the name of the great sea that surround us
We enter into prayer.

For the living, who still breathe the air and walk among the
trees, we sing:
We who now go unto sleep,
Be it that we in health shall waken;
Or if death be to us in the death-sleep,
Be it that we awaken in the Otherworld,
O Gods of death, we in peace shall waken;
    Be it on Thine own beloved arms,
    O God of transformation, that we in knowledge shall
wake.

For newly dead, those who have died and gone to the
Otherworld before us,[in the honor of [names]], we sing
Safeguard those who have gone before us,
O Gods and Psychopomps, lead members of this household
to-night,
    Themselves and their means and their fame,
Deliver them from pain, from distress, from harm,
    From the fruits of envy and of enmity.
And show them the way to the Land of Youth,
        Guide them to the Isle of Apples
Celebrate with them in the Land Beyond the Ninth Wave.

For the Holy and Mighty Dead, who know what it is to be
beyond the Veil, we sing:
You souls who dwell on the Isles of the Blessed,
You Powers beyond the Veil of Death

You who guide us beyond our understanding
All who show us the lands beyond this land
   Be with us this day/night and encircle us
   That no harm, no evil shall us befall.
Whilst the body is dwelling in the sleep and waking,
Our souls are reaching to land, sea, and sky,
Be the support and tribe behind and before us,
   Early and late, night and day,
   Early and late, night and day.

In the name of the land that supports us,
In the name of the sky vaulted above us,
In the name of the great sea that surrounds us,
We enter into the world.

Second Office of the Dead

In the name of the land that supports us,
In the name of the sky vaulted above us,
And in the name of the great sea that surrounds us,
We enter into prayer.

We all live and we will all die. This is a part of living in this glorious world. There is a cycle of life and death and as much as we may watch summer move to winter and summer again, we will all face our own winters and the dying of our own suns.

Donne, the first to die and enter the Otherworld,
We honor You and ask for you to be with us
Not because we are near death
But because we will join you one day
You are our kinsman
Your house is one we will pass through
Prepare us for our journey
And let us know that this is not an end
But a beginning
Be our friend, our kinsman, and our guide.

[If appropriate: Today we gather to honor (name).]

Although you have transversed the veil and sailed the sea through the mists to the Holy Isles, there is and always will be a path of light back so that we might know one another again and so that your loved ones may honor you.

(Name) Find liberation now, be strong as you always were, be proud of who you have been, know that you will be mourned and honored, that you have loved and are beloved.

Move now beyond form, flowing like the sea, dancing in moonlight, luminous as the stars in the night sky.

Pass the mists, enter without fear or pain. Return to the womb of life to sleep in the great cauldron of rebirth. Be forever blessed for you are and will always be our family, joined by blood and spirit for eternity.

Mighty Dead, long dead, ancestors, we invoke you now, with light and with song
You who remain in the Isles of the Blessed
Who revel in the Plain of Apples and Isle of Women
We call on your now to support us and join us
We ask for wisdom
We ask for your faith
We ask for your presence and support
We make these offerings to you
We honor you
Someday we will join you
Guide us, teach us, and keep us in the palms of your hands

In the name of the land that supports us,
In the name of the sky vaulted above us,
And in the name of the great sea that surrounds us,
We enter into the world.

Our Holy Days

These are specific prayers written for the neo-pagan eight holidays of the wheel of the year. As mentioned earlier in this text, these prayers are not an inherent sanction for the modern esoteric Wheel of Year as the only way to celebrate holidays and the passage of time. However, the fire festivals have strong histories in Celtic nations and the solar holidays obviously mark the turning of the seasons and, thus, are a valid pattern of celebration.

As singular prayers and not offices unto themselves, which will be a future book, these prayers can be added to morning and evening offices, as suites a practitioner. Each monastic practitioner should also be free to add additional prayers and offices as suits their personal needs. For the Samhain evening office and spring equinox morning office, as mentioned previously, the office of dying and office of healing, respectively, can be added in addition to the specific prayer commemorating the holy day.

Samhain

Bless, O Three-Fold Powers
Everything within our dwelling or in our possession
All kine and crops, all flocks and corn
From Hallow Eve to Beltane Eve
With goodly progress and gentle blessing
From sea to sea and every river mouth
      From wave to waves, and base of waterfall
Be the Powers taking possession of all to us belonging
Be the sure of protecting us in truth
O satisfy our souls in this thin time
And shield our loved ones, living and dead
Bless everything and everyone
Of this little household by our side.

Winter Solstice

On this, the darkest of nights,
May the greatest blessings of light be upon us,
O Shining Ones,
O powers and ancestors and spirits
Sain us and shield us in the deep darkness
Of night and winter and cold
Light within us and light without us
Light to guide us on the road
Light to always guide us home.

Imbolc

Here comes to our assistance,
Pale fair Brigid;
With ewes bearing lambs,
With the cows bearing calves,
With the earth bearing green and white,
With the sunlight slowly growing
Assist us, foster-mother,
Ancestor and Power, bringer of spring
Without gold, without corn, without kine,
We come to you as foster-children,
Aid us O Brid!

Spring Equinox

Pastures smooth, long and spreading
Grassy meads beneath our feet
The friendship of powers, gods, and spirits to always lead us
home
To the field of the fountains,
       To the field of the many waters,
Closed be every pit and trench to us
Smoothed be every knoll and crag to us
Cosy every exposure and high place to us
Beside and on the cold mountains.
Glory in the life of this equinox day!
Glory in the green of the earth this day!
Give thanks to the ancestors, who lived before us!
Give thanks to the powers of earth, bringing forth life!
Give thanks to the Shining Ones, leading us today!

Beltane

O night of bonfires and O day of dancing
This is the night malign and day benign
To send the sheep on prosperity
To send cow on calf
To put the web in the warp
To set the coracle on the sea
To hang the flag on the staff
To hunt the stag on the heights
To send herds to pasture
To make prayer efficacious,
To make the day for our beloveds.
O Gods of the sea, land, and sky,
Enrich the ground,
Shower on us food,
Give us blessings this day and all days.

Summer Solstice

The sun, victorious in the sky
We make our circuit under your shield
O Manannan of the white shield!
We make our circuit
On the machair, on the meadow
On the cold heathery hill of summer
Though we should travel the ocean
And the hard globe of the world
Among hardy and wild places
Be at peace with us
With our horses, with cattle
With the crops growing in the field
Everything on high or low,
Every furnishing and flock,
Be at peace, be at peace, be at peace.

Lughnasadh

On this the feast memorial of Lugh,
Lugh of the Long Arm, Lugh Samildánach
We cut a handful of the young corn
We ground in a quern
We bake it on a fan of sheep-skin
And we share it with our people.
In peace, in flocks,
In righteousness of heart
In labor, in love,
In wisdom, and in mercy
O Powers above and spirits with us,
Ancestors before us
Preserve us!

Autumn Equinox

On the feast of the equinox at the rise of the sun,
And the back of the ear of corn to the east,
We will go forth with our sickles under our arms,
And we will reap the cut, the first act.
We will let our sickles down
While the fruitful ear is in our grasp,
We will raise our eyes upwards,
We give thanks to the spirits of the earth,
For the growing crops of the ground.
We give thanks to the ancestors before us
Who taught us the art of the harvest.
We give thanks to the Shining Ones,
Who are ever before us.

Help me to journey beyond the familiar
and into the unknown.
Give me the faith to leave old ways
and break fresh ground with You.
O mysterious Powers, I trust You
to be stronger than each storm within me.
I will trust in the darkness and know
that my times, even now, are in Your hands.
Tune my spirit to the music of the Otherworld,
and somehow, make my willingness answer to You.
(Prayer of St Brendan, adapted)

OUR CONCLUSION

These prayers and offices are not offered as dogmatic prayers that define the office and days of those who follow a monastic way of life. Asceticism can follow many forms and what has been laid forth in this text is only one way. This is the pattern followed by my household and the Fellowship of the Nine Waves. Others may find different paths. I encourage those who are so called to explore global forms of monasticism, especially those associated with their Gods, Powers, and spirits. We must always honor our own distinct callings.

This is, however, a distinct way of communing with the Divine. This is the manner by which we mark our days, our seasons, and our hours according to the Fellowship of the Nine Waves. While the Office of the Hours and the Offices of Healing and Dying may be formulaic, we all make them distinct in our own way. We will all pray to our own Deities and Powers and we will all uniquely commit ourselves to this way of life.

The asceticism called for this text is one of rigorous prayer and mindful living, rather than bodily mortification or intentional poverty, which may be more familiar to those who have studied monasticism. This is not to say that mortification and poverty have no place an ascetic monastic practice, but that I do not believe them to be inherently necessary. If it is a part of an individual's practice, that is completely between the practitioner and the Powers who called them.

There is something to be said for the asceticism of even practicing the Office of Hours in our current secular culture. We, especially in the United States, live in a culture that deprecates the spiritual and religious. We culturally believe that the religious and devotional are, somehow, intellectually lesser than those who are secular. The cultural stereotype of the illiterate Bible thumper is easily transferable to the polytheistic devotionalist or monastic, even as both are tied up in cultural stereotypes related to education, class, patriotism, counterculturalism, and the use of science as a post-Enlightenment replacement for the morality and spirituality.

This is not the place to dive into the problems of replacing religion and spirituality with science, but it is important to note that religion and science answer different philosophical questions. They are both important. The religious among us should follow science and honor what science teaches us. However, science does not and cannot replace religion and spirituality. They occupy different places in our intellectual world.

We should honor the intellectual and scientific research that educates us about the world around us, however science is not ethics nor is it morality. Science without valid morality and ethics is what gives us the extensive use of lobotomies in the twentieth century, the Tuskegee Experiments, the plutonium injections of the Manhattan Project, the history of Henrietta Lacks, and many others. Science, without morality, exploits the vulnerable and supports the status quo. Exalting it unto itself is inherently dangerous.

Thus a Celtic monastic practice fundamentally disrupts the status quo of both the secular institutions of Western and Occidental culture and the understanding that religion and spirituality will be of the mainstream, often monotheistic faiths. This does not mean that we engage in our practice in order to disrupt their worldview or because we are counterculture. We engage in our faith and practices because we are called to them, but, by that calling, we are separate and different.

Because we are different, because we engage in a unique spirituality, because we are a part of Celtic culture which if not a dominant culture, we will inherently experience opposition. This is okay and can even be a source of validity. We are different. We can even use different prayers of hours, if a practitioner is called to do so. But we are called to these practices and these cultures and that is the important thing.

Practice. Pray. Offer. Pray. Give thanks. Pray. Be silent. Pray. Commune. Pray. Give libation. Pray. Make burnt offering. Pray. Isolate oneself. Pray. Read. Pray. Listen. Pray. Be silent. Pray. Sing the office of the dead. Pray. Be mindful. Pray. Be constant. Pray. Be devoted. Pray. Work. Pray.

And learn this, if nothing else has been understood: pray.

Prayer is the mechanism by which we communicate with ourselves and with the Holy. Whether is is by meditation, thanksgiving, petition, consecration, intercession, or imprecation, we know, as polytheists, that we can communicate with the Divine, the Holy, and the Otherworldly. We can also, by this communication and by our cultural and social history, know our social ethics and morality. These are the identifications by which we can separate ourselves.

We ought to be part of our secular worlds and our dominant cultures, but when we engage in a Celtic polytheistic monasticism, we keep ourselves in a separate culture. We need to bring these Celtic polytheistic monastic values, ethics, morals, and ideals to the forefront and make them important not just in our personal lives, but socially, communally, and collectively. We are different and that is good.

Oisín Doyle is a priest and one of the founders of The Fellowship of the Nine Waves, a monastic Celtic polytheistic church. He brings a knowledge and experience of several contemplative faith paths, including Roman Catholicism, Buddhism, and modern paganism. He is the director of the liturgical and clerical programs for the Fellowship of the Nine Waves. As part of this role, he is a writer on both LGBT and pagan topics, a visual artist, and researcher. When he is not engaged in his work, he often be found with his nose in a book in suburban Philadelphia, where he lives with his partner and their very sassy dog. He can be reached at fellowshipoftheninewaves@gmail.com.

The Fellowship of the Nine Waves
◆ a celtic pagan church ◆

The Fellowship of the Nine Waves is a modern monastic Celtic polytheistic church, founded in the United States. As a monastic fellowship creating a 21st century pathway of silence and contemplation, we are an open tradition that embraces members from all walks of life. We are a monastic Fellowship promoting a 21st century Paganism with a focus on the environment, vulnerability, and a direct connection with the Gods. For information about membership, events, and ordination - fellowshipoftheninewaves@gmail.com.

Made in the USA
Monee, IL
22 March 2023

30342318R00080